SOVIET AND CHINESE PERSONALITIES

Wilhelm S. Heiliger

University Press of America™

University Press of America, Inc.
4720 Boston Way, Lanham, MD 20801

Printed in the United States of America
ISBN: 0-8191-1213-5 (Case)
0-8191-1214-3 (Perfect)

Library of Congress Catalog Card Number: 80-1383

FOR LINDA

TABLE OF CONTENTS

PREFACE

The 20th century is characterized not only by revolutions, world wars, massive elimination of peoples, nationalistic upheavals and political regroupings from fascist military regimes to revolutionary Marxist government concepts and vice versa, but also by ideological change and by the search for new value concepts and world order.

In Russia, the October Revolution of 1917 initiated a transformation process of basic human values, as well as political and ideological guidelines, and subsequently brought about the creation of new personality models and structures; these models are seen as important parameters of societal change and for implementing government policies and doctrines.

A further mass-political and ideological campaign during the 20th century was initiated in Nazi Germany, where the cult of the leadership personality (Fuhrerpersonlichkeit) was created as the basis for Nazi mythological and religious value system of the Third Reich.

Mao Tse-tung organized the proletarian Revolution and established the People's Republic of China in 1949. Again, the basis for his revolutionary actions is ideological and intellectual value transformations; they are geared towards change of human existence and personality orientation as a tenet of Chinese Communist behavior.

However, our knowledge of contemporary Soviet and Chinese personality structures and personal value modifications is limited and has not been a subject of thorough scholarly evaluation. This study evaluates specific aspects of current Soviet scholarly research within the sociology and psychology of personality as related to the scientific-technological revolution in the USSR. The publications analyzed and evaluated were published by various Soviet University presses, as well as presses of different regional Academies of Sciences of the USSR.

It is the intention of this study to portray critical Soviet personality evaluations as well as desired personality models, regardless of their actual correctness or application within the Soviet society. The presentation of Soviet personality models is based on Soviet self-criticism of social conditions and on theoretical experimentation within the changing Marxist doctrine. Each chapter represents a description and analysis of personality assessments and of actual or desired personality characteristics as seen from the Soviet perspective.

Western publications pertinent to Soviet personality structures have been organized. However, most of the Western publications related to Soviet personality models and value transformations were written during the period of the Cold War, and therefore reflect the political realities of that period; they do not reflect current Soviet scholarly concepts and configurations of personality research within Soviet psychology, sociology, and ideology.

The second part of the study describes contemporary personality structures and models within the People's Republic of China. The scholarly literature analyzed and evaluated has been published primarily in the United States and in the People's Republic of China. Again, the intention is to portray the Chinese Communist personality models as seen from the Chinese perspective, rather than through politically indoctrinated interpretations and Western perception of communist doctrines and value concepts. A comparative Soviet-Chinese evaluation of personality structures and value concepts concludes the study.

I would like to thank Professor Paul Cocks of Stanford University and Professor Josef Brozek of Lehigh University for their professional advice and criticism. In addition, I owe special thanks to Bill Widen of Stanford University and Linda Munn of San Jose State University for reading the entire manuscript.

Stanford, California
June 1980
Wilhelm S. Heiliger

L I S T O F T A B L E S

22. Organizational qualities of leaders of production enterprises evaluated by their staff.
23. Professional qualities of leaders of production enterprises evaluated by their staff.
24. Human qualities of leaders of production enterprises evaluated by their staff.
25. Professional qualifications of Soviet educators.
26. Leadership qualities and personality characteristics of educators evaluated by students.
27. What character traits should a worker, foreman and engineer possess?
28. Confucian behavior patterns.
29. Personality characteristics of Chinese revolutionaries.
30. Competing value systems as they apply to the organization of scientific activities.

A. HISTORICAL PERSPECTIVE OF PERSONALITY CONCEPTS

1. GENERAL PERSONALITY CONCEPTS

The word ' person ' is derived from the Latin word ' persona ', which originally described the mask of an actor. The meaning of the term changed about 60 B.C., when Cicero used it in different intellectual interpretations, as for example, the function or the role one person plays in life, or the impression one person makes upon others; further interpretations include personal characteristics, as well as the prestige and dignity of persons. To represent one's own person before the court of law was a privilege only for non-slaves, according to the Codex Justinianius. The legal person distinguished itself from the thing (Latin res), in being able to make decisions for oneself and in being able to determine one's own actions. In the 6th century, Boethius defined the term person as ' undividable substance of the rational being '; this definition was used through the period of scholasticism.

John Locke (1690), Ch. Wolff (1734), J.F. Herbart (1824) emphasized the knowledge and self-confidence of the ' person ' within different conditions and time periods as one and the same value. Modern psychological terminology rarely uses the word person. The term ' person ' has been replaced by the neutral definition " personality ". The concept of the personality was used quite frequently during the 18th century. The concept was formed in connection with the humanistic ideals of the European classics (Goethe, Schiller). Personality was used then as the highest goal of self-realization of man through education. The individualistic intellectual tendencies of the 19th century treated the concept of personality positively; however, they specifically distinguished the concept of the personality as belonging to an individual. In comparison with the 18th and 19th century, the concept of personality is used in the 20th century in connection with the influence of the environment and the principle of equality.

The Concept of Personality

A personality is an individual human being, who is able to develop his talents as a person with regard to a distinct form of individual features and original value characteristics. In comparison to the general structural concept of the person (persona), personality appears as a concrete individual, with particular features of personal expression. Accordingly, every moral and responsible human being is a person, but not necessarily a personality. On the other hand, personality is perceived as a center and core of the person. The concept of the personality contains individual characteristics (the structure of spiritual talents) and is closely related with the concept of character. Therefore, The concept of the personality is subjected to specific research on personality structures. The concept of character is perceived rather as a static-structural element, in comparison with the personality, which is analyzed as a dynamic moment of realization and action. The ethical value of the personality, its radiating power, is based on the strength and consequence of its own character, which is connected with the realization of certain normative conception.

Research on Personality Concepts

The origins of the psychology of the personality are in the American ' personology ' or ' personalistics ' (initiated by W. Stern and H.A. Murray) that flourished after the Second World War and which replaced the European school of characterology.

Since the beginning of the 1940's, research on personality was directed at illuminating the dynamic cohesion of the individual organization of the human psyche. Certain aspects of psychoanalysis and depth psychology have been applied within personality research, as for example the growth process during early childhood, repetitive and typical behavior traits through the biological method (Charlotte Buhler), including some aspects of social-psychological research, primarily in the United States, which attempted to explore the human being in connection with specific social structures and cultural behavior models. Also included were psychodiagnostic techniques utilizing tests and questionnaires.

R. Heiss (1947) and H. Thomae (1951) from Germany and G.W. Allport and D.J. Dollard from the United States, emphasized longitudinal aspects in evaluating the personality structure.

Cross studies among depth psychologists, ethnologists, anthropologists and sociologists developed in the U.S. different social-psychological theories of personality. The core of such research is seen in socially oriented approaches and actions related to adaptations and developments of group-dynamics. The factor theories of the personality were developed by Ch. Spearman (1935), J.P. Geilford (1940), R.B. Cattel (1950), and H.J. Eysenck (1953). Eysenck differentiated four sections of the personality in his theory: the cognitive section (intelligence), the conative section (character), the affective section (temperament), and the somatic section (organism). His goal is the construction of a mathematical model of the organization of the personality. However, Allport is the major opponent of mathematical models of the personality, claiming that it is an artificial construction, without the required internal cohesion. The factor-analysis applied to personality produces the same results as, for example, the typology with its formalistic and hypothetical means (A. Wellek). Since 1955, hypnotism has been used as an experimental tool in securing characteristic features of reality, especially by providing the proof of the ' core-structure ' of the personality.

2. WESTERN INTERPRETATIONS OF THE SOVIET PERSONALITY

a. Soviet Literature as a Transformer of Human Values

The aim of the Communist Party of the USSR is to develop a personality model which will produce men who are multi-faceted, and easily malleable. The communist education and artistic creativity is not only concerned with ideological transformations; it includes the raising of the productivity on the basis of improved technology, shortening the working day, communist methods of labor organizations, raising the material standards of the masses, enlisting public opinion in the drive for better health services and more harmonious living conditions, the development of a specialist and general education, and the general stimulation of initiative by the masses in all spheres of economic, communal and public life in the USSR.

One of the most effective means used to form a socialist personality in the Soviet Union is its educational system, as well as the fine arts. " In the development and enrichment of the culture of a socialist society, an important part is played by literature and the arts, which actively facilitate the formation of the man of Communist society..."(1) Literature functions as a socio-economic transformer and modernizer. In the theoretical framework of socialist realism, literature has been transformed into a detailed expression of the official value system. Writers have been charged specifically with the creation of two literary stereotypes: the positive and negative hero. They could be treated as personifications of good and evil serving as models of behavior. Such models are also highly functional for the requirements of a rapidly industrializing society.

The new man in the Soviet society is supposed to have internalized the notion that the most desirable behavior pattern consists of responsiveness to the commands and cues of the regime. " The stability of the Soviet-type of totalitarianism and regime has, so far, rested primarily on the control of behavior and not on ultimate values."(2) Personal relationships are a prime example, which,by virtue of their diffuseness and inherent privacy, are difficult to bring under satisfactory political-institutional control. This is one reason why literature was called upon to penetrate the corners of privacy and to provide guidance through models of behavior. " From the sociological point of view, socialist realism is a politically supported carrier of the ideal patterns devised by the ruling groups, disseminated in a monolithic fashion. Its main features are tendentiousness, optimism, simplification, the politization of conflicts and typicality."(3) Harold Swayze summarizes the concept of literary control and social development within the USSR in saying, " ... that the Soviet regime has displayed an acute awareness of the vast influence that works of art exert precisely because of their claims on emotions. The regime has far outdone other totalitarian systems striving to guide these potentialities into desired channels, to foster a literature of a certain kind and a certain content, one that will play an active role in indoctrinating the masses and integrating the individual into the social whole."(4) Jurgen Ruhle quotes Makarenko, in connection with the education of the Soviet man. " To educate a person means to create for him the perspectives of his journey through life, where he can find the joys of the tomorrow." (5) Eng-Liedmeier concludes ..." that a great change has come about in the portrayal of the seemingly perfect Soviet man. What is shown in the ealier periods is a lack of genuine revolutionary zeal, of personal courage and initiative. It is not the Party to blame for this, for it appears that it is the Party itself which partly consists of people of their kind." (6) Herman Ermolaev describes the process of value transformation within Soviet literature as follows; " As Party members of conviction, the Onlinguardists were concerned above all with advancing communism; they believed that its triumph required a thorough psychological re-education of man within the framework of the cultural revolution. This is the chief reason why they advocated psychological realism as the most effective literary contribution to the building of socialism and communism." (7) Kultschinskiy's analysis of the literary impact on the personality structure points out the relationship between the description of the literary character of the personality and the psychological characteristics of the personality. " The concrete personality forms the major subject in literature. Literature contributes significantly to the psychology of the personality and to the psychology of character." (8)

b. Western Psychological Interpretations of the Soviet Personality

In his book, Stalin and the Uses of Psychology, Robert Tucker points out that the state-directed man bears significant resemblance to persons in the neurotic condition known to modern psychiatry as self-alienation. " The self-alienated person lacks a clear sense of personal identity and the inner directive powers normally associated with it, such as the faculty of active choice, independent decisions, awareness of his own feelings and opinions, the urge and capacity to pursue his own goals and satisfaction, etc... the state-directed man is, above all, a person bereft of autonomous inner motivations and dependent for the determining of his conduct upon verbal cues given from without. He lacks a real self capable of going its independent way and forming its own values." (9) Raymond Bauer develops a doctrine of consciousness of modern Soviet psychology; he emphasizes that Soviet pedagogy holds the principle that it is "... the conscious personality of man, his conscious behavior, and his discipline that are to be moulded."(10) L. Prokupek defined the Marxist man as " The product of historical development." Z. Barbu approached the Soviet personality concept from the psychoanalytical aspect.

" He, the man under Communism, is not allowed to think and to feel about himself as a value, or as an end, but as a means in the structure of the Party. Consequently he suffers from an incapacity to regard his own connection with things as having any intrinsic value whatsoever. The Party systematically destroys, by the technique of deracination any emotional couche and any nest of warm feelings which, at one moment or the other, an individual may build up in his intimate contact with things and persons... We can assume, however, that the communist civilization contains the basic conditions of a new type of personality whose behavior is basically determined by his group awareness. He can, therefore, be described as a collective personality."(12) Handley Cantril charaterizes the Soviet personality being formed under totalitarian conditions and circumstances. " Nearly all people are like children in that they need to be led and can be led by hand, being conditioned to ask no questions about where they are going..."(13) This assumption essentially denies the value quality inherent in spontaneous experience. In operational terms, this means that essentially an individual must have party or state permission in order to get into contact with many of his deep emotions and feelings. Frank Meyer elaborates a concept of a totalitarian type of personality; his approach is motivated by ideological and political value perceptions of the Soviet man, rather than by scholarly analysis of psychological value concepts. " The ideal type of communist is a man in whom all individual, emotional and unconscious elements have been reduced to a minimum and subjected to the control of an iron will, informed by the supple intellect."(14) Rene Fueloep-Miller examines the Soviet development of mind transformation under communist control and guidance in connection with prehistoric primitive man. " The impersonal collective man whose development required not the slightest moral independence, but merely blind mechanically obedience, thus formed the ideal of the Soviet communist. The individual is no more himself; he has become an automaton with no will of his own. In Le Bon's judgement, " man, by adherence to a mass, descends in the scale of civilization; although, in his isolation, he was perhaps a cultivated individual, once merged in the mass, he will become a barbarous creature of instinct."(15) John Kosa analyzed in his study, <u>Two Generations of Soviet Man</u>, basic psychological concepts of Soviet man. He concludes in saying that " man has to satify both the individual and the collective superego, and it is no small task to serve two masters. The collective superego may make a demand which is contrary to his individual norms; it may severely restrict his freedom to pursue his own goals; it may require much self-sacrifice and abnegation. The collective superego contains the goals and values in a group and, through them, regulates cooperation and competition." (16) Robert Tucker compared the creation of the new personality of Soviet man with the conditioning process of the Pavlovian model. " Man had to be understood as a being whose character and conduct are controlled at every step by the conditioning process, whose every psychic act is a reflex. The Pavlovian model of the personality is seen as a shift from an ' inner-directed type ', whose character operates as an autonomous determining force in life, to an ' other-directed type ', whose behavior is guided by signals received from outside. In the Soviet version, however, the sole source of the signals to which the ' other-directed ' person responds is the state." (17) The essay by Alexander Inkeles, Eugenie Hanfmann and Helen Beier, on modal personality and the re-adjustment of the Soviet sociological system, is based on a questionnaire study undertaken at Harvard University Russian Research Center. The findings dwell on the need of the Russian people for affiliation of the personality to certain institutions and groups. A further strong drive of the Russian personality is the desire for individual autonomy; the negative aspects reveal a lack of well-developed defensive structures of the Russian people in relationship to the social structure of the society and their political institutions. Inkeles evaluated other aspects of the Russian personality, such as: the relationship towards authority, self-esteem, emotional aliveness, awareness of the other as a distinct entity, freedom and spontaneity in criticism, the bi-modality of an assertive-passive pattern of strivings as compared to the American people. " The picture of the Russian modal personality patterns which emerge from our study is highly congruent with the traditional or classic picture of the Russian character reported in history, literature, and current travelers account..."(18) Raymond Bauer supported the general thesis that personality characteristics develop as a result of the incorporation by the child of certain aspects of his social activity. The goal of developing a new aspect of contemporary Soviet psychology lies in ' desirable behavior ', or ' practical importance ', which can be manipulated, motivated and indoctrinated by higher authorities. The personality structure within the Soviet human value system still survives in ' functioning attitudes ' of the individual, rather than in building up personal value orientations and intellectual-creative abilities. Soviet psychology is training people for obedience and subjugation as a tool for political manipulation of social and intellectual development. " The practical value of these methods is instrumental in shaping a soul-less, mechanized, automated reflex theory, which functions and responds to authoritative inputs."(19)

Robert Magidoff discusses the idea that Soviet psychologists have added to inheritance and environment two universally accepted factors that determine personality: the factors of training and self-training. " The Soviet man is possessed with inner discipline and inner drive that enable him to be in a perpetual state of self-mobilization. He is constantly struggling with his own shortcomings: weakness of character, overconfidence, ignorance, self-indulgance, complacency, and ideological backwardness. "(20) Rubinsteyn is insistent that personality is made up of different levels. It includes not only individual, more or less varible, characteristics which have been aquired in the course of phylogenesis and which are common to all men. " Among the multiple characteristics of man's personality, those appear as most specifically personal which condition the socially significant activities of man. It is these characteristics which make him a person, in the true sense of the word. A man is a person through his relationship to society. The person, therefore, is the ' unit ' in the system of social relations. Personality is primarily a social not a psychological concept."(21) Seve Lucian elaborated a Western Marxist approach towards the contemporary Soviet personality analysis in the concept of historical materialism in relationship to basic processes of individual life and the formation of the personality of all mankind. " The personality is transforming the nature and culture of civilization, without knowing that also social processes are being transformed by culture and nature within the historical and social development of the personality. The major human conflict lies within the diversity and complexity of personality actualization." (22) Wilhelm Arnold related the Soviet personality to the historical perspective and to current ideological guidelines within the social sciences. " Personality has a manifold meaning within the Soviet characterology; it relates for example, to the inner stability of personality, the ability to communicate with others and the ability to develop self-oriented values of life, the ego-relationship, the evaluation of one-self. The new Soviet man however, is the task of a value oriented psychology of personality."(23)

SUMMARY

Soviet literature, as a transformer of human values and personality concepts, has strongly advocated ideological and political views since the October Revolution in 1917. The aim of the Soviet literature was, and still is, to develop personality models which will form a multi-faceted developed communist citizen. Literature functions as a socio-economic transformer of the Soviet society. Soviet literature and its concepts of socialist realism were transformed into an expression of the official value system. P. Hollander characterizes Soviet literature as a tool which controls human behavior for the totalitarian regime. Harold Swayze sees Soviet literature playing an active role in indoctrinating the masses and integrating the individual into the social whole. Ermolaev describes the process of value transformation within Soviet literature, where a thorough psychological re-education of man within the framework of the cultural revolution is required. Literature further contributes to the psychology of the personality and to the psychology of character (Kultschinskij).

Robert Tucker analyzed the psychological aspects of the Soviet personality. He relates a state-directed man with an alienated personality, which lacks an inner directed power, such as active choice, the ability to make independent decisions, etc. Raymond Bauer refers to the conscious behavior of the Soviet man which has to be moulded. Zevedei Barbu characterized the personality structure as a personality whose behavior is basically determined by group-awareness. Handley Cantril and Frank Meyer interpreted the Soviet personality as formed under totalitarian conditions. Rene Fueloep-Miller examined the development of mind transformation under communist control in connection with prehistoric primitive man. A. Inkeles compares the Soviet modal personality structure with the traditional picture of the Russian character reported in history. The majority of Western scholars of Soviet affairs see the significance of the Soviet personality formation in ' functioning attitudes ' of individuals under totalitarian control mechanisms and totalitarian value perceptions.

R E F E R E N C E S

1. C. Vaugham James, Socialist Realism, Origins and Theory. St. Martins Press, New York, 1974, p. 94. (With reference to the 21st Party Congress of the CPSU, Speech of N.S. Khrushchev).

2. Paul Hollander, Models of Behavior in Stalinist Literature: A Case Study of Totalitarian Values and Controls. In: American Sociological Review, 1964, p. 364.

3. J. Levy, Jr., The Structure of Society. Princeton University Press, 1952, pp. 123-125.

4. Harold Swayze, Political Control of Literature in the USSR. Harvard University Press, 1964, pp.23-24.

5. Jurgen Ruhle, Literatur und Revolution. Die Schriftsteller und der Kommunismus. Kiepenheuer & Witsch Verlag, Koln, 1960, p. 97.

6. A.M. Van der Eng-Liedmeier, Soviet Literary Characters. An Introduction into the Portrayal of Soviet Man in Russian Prose. 1917-1953. Mouton, Co. 1959, p. 160.

7. Herman Ermolaev, Soviet Literary Theories, 1917-1934. The Genesis of Socialist Realism. University of California Press, Publications in Modern Philology, Vol. 69, 1963, p. 67.

8. A. Kultschinskiy, Die Marxistisch-sowjetische Konzeption des Menschen im Lichte der westlichen Psychologie. Institut der UDSSR, Munchen, Serie I. No. 32, 1956, p. 94.

9. Robert C. Tucker, Stalin and the Uses of Psychology. U.S. Air Force Project. RAND Research Memorandum, RM-1441, March 10, 1955, p. 75.

10. Raymond A. Bauer, The New Man in Soviet Psychology. Harvard University Press, Cambridge, 1952, p. 132.

11. Ladislav Prokupek, Der Mensch im Marxismus. Jugenddienst Verlag, Wuppertal, 1970, p. 13.

12. Zevedei Barbu, Democracy and Dictatorship and their Psychology and Pattern of Life. The Communist Type of Personality. pp. 255-256.

13. Handley Cantril, Soviet Leaders and Mastery over Man. Rutgers University Press, 1960, p. 23.

14. Frank S. Meyer, The Moulding of Communists. A Harvest Book, 1961, p. 25.

15. Rene Fueloep-Miller, The Mind and Face of Bolshevism. An Examination of Cultural Life in Soviet Russia. Harper Torchbooks, New York, 1965, p. 19.

16. John Kosa, Two Generations of Soviet Man. A Study in the Psychology of Communism. The University of North Caroline Press, 1962, p. 20.

17. Robert C. Tucker, The Soviet Political Mind. Stalin and the Uses of Psychology. Praeger Paperbacks, New York, 1963, p. 108.

18. Alexander Inkeles, Social Change in Soviet Russia. A Clarion Book; Simon and Schuster, New York, 1971, pp. 131-132.

19. Raymond A. Bauer, Ed., Some Views on Soviet Psychology. Published by the American Psychological Association, Inc., Washington, D.C. 1962, p. 70.

20. Robert Magidoff, The Kremlin vs. The People. Doubleday and Company, Inc., New York, 1953, p. 226.

21. T.R. Payne, S.L. Rubinsteyn and the Philosophical Foundation of Soviet Psychology. D. Reidel Publishing Co., p. 138.

22. Seve Lucian, Marxisme et Theorie de la Personalite. Editions sociales, Paris, p. 195.

23. Wilhelm Arnold, Personlichkeit. In: Sowjetsystem und Demokratische Gesellschaft. Eine Vergleichende Enzyklopadie, Herder Verlag, Freiburg, 1966.

3. POLITICAL REINFORCEMENT OF THE SOVIET PERSONALITY

Since the October Revolution in 1917, the Communist Party of the USSR has been implementing a re-education program to shape the ideal Soviet personality and a new human value system, based on the Marxist-Leninist ideological doctrine. Its main goals have been to create personality models for their citizens, to restructure moral and ideological values, to develop a new psychology for the Soviet society, and above all else, to create a new Soviet man.

Initially a new mentality structure was introduced through various governmental control mechanisms, which enabled the Soviet government to better manipulate the behavior of its citizens and indirectly force them into a framework of party obedience. Such psychological and educational tools provided the Communist Party of the USSR with stricter control over private emotions of individuals, as well as their personal desires, aspirations, and finally, their intimate lives. The reshaping process of the societal structure in the USSR through mass-psychological, ideological, educational and sociological means and the creation of group-oriented living conditions, represents one of the major transformations of human value systems during the 20th century.

The contemporary importance of the Soviet personality development was emphasized in the speeches of Party Secretary General of the CPSU, Leonid Brezhnev, at the 24th and 25th Party Congress of the CPSU, in 1971 and 1976.
" Comrades! The power of our (Party) machinery lies in the consciousness of the masses. The Party takes the responsibility of educating the people in communist consciousness, the adaptability, the willpower and the understanding of creating communism. During the present period, the Party is emphasizing the problems of the ideological education of the masses, the problems of creating a New Man, an honest builder of communism; these efforts are a major part of our Party's work." (1)

As the result of the 23rd Party Congress of the CPSU in 1966, action was taken by the Central Committee in August 1967 through its resolution " On Measures for Further Developing the Social Sciences and Strengthening Their Role in Communist Construction." The resolution noted that in the era of transition from capitalism to socialism, Marxist-Leninist theory and the role of the social sciences have become increasingly important: "... intensification of creative work in the sphere of theory is imperative to strengthen the political, economic and cultural cooperation of the socialist countries."The resolution of the CPSU proceeded to list specific tasks to improve the situation in the fields of philosophy, economics, scientific communism, sociology, cybernetics, the management system, the two world systems approach, and the communication sciences.

Scholars of the social sciences were given more leeway with regard to developing new scientific approaches and research methods in forming contemporary class consciousness and a socialist human value system. The loosening of tight ideological controls and guidelines enabled the Soviet social scientists to develop experimental research in transforming and changing contemporary socialist society. Therefore, the ideological priorities are in the process of decline within the Soviet society. One can clearly see the tendency on the part of the decision-making elite of the Central Committee of the CPSU to restructure the traditional totalitarian control mechanisms, with an attitude of change in reorienting the human value system. The new guidelines of the Central Committee are more concerned with management capabilities and production growth of enterprises, as well as individual responsibility of Party officials and managers of production enterprises, than with tenets of Marxism-Leninism. The research directions of the Soviet social sciences in the area of human behavior and personality modification are geared toward experimentation and the search for new and contemporary personality structures which will adjust more successfully to the scientific-technological revolution within the Soviet society and within general social developments. Social change is a significant factor in forming the technocratic-management and elite group personality.

REFERENCES

1. XXV s'ezd kommunisticheskoy partii Sovetskogo Soyuza, Otchet Tsentral'nogo komiteta KPSS i ocherednye zadachi partii; doklad general'nogo sekretarya TsK KPSS tovarishcha L.I.Brezhneva, 24 Fevralya 1976 goda; III. Partiya v usloviyakh razvitogo sotsializma. 2. Ideyno-vospitatel'naya rabota partii. Pravda, 25 Fevralya 1976 g. p. 8.

4. HISTORICAL PERSPECTIVE OF THE SOVIET PERSONALITY

N. Vasilyev published a book in 1906 entitled The Ten Commandements of the Social-Democrats; the study is a description of revolutionary values for workers and the general proletariat; it is at the same time a guidebook for workers who are still outside organized movements, as well as guidelines for proletarian tasks and goals. The following ten principles on the conduct of revolutionaries, presented through the policies of social-democrats, indicate the beginning of an intellectual transformation process and the restructuring of the existing political and personal value system. The personality adjustments and changes, as proposed by Vasilyev, with regard to a proletarian personality, are as follows:

1. Remember that you are a poor man and that all poor men are your brothers.
2. Do not sell your soul to the capitalists, who buy your body and the bodies of your brothers.
3. Do not forget that the poor are as an ocean, while the rich are only a few; believe that victory is not difficult if a ray of light enters the ignorant heads of your brothers and sisters.
4. Educate yourself and educate your sisters and brothers.
5. Sacrifice your life for them, if necessary.
6. Unite your sisters and brothers in unions.
7. Serve not dissent, but serve conciliation between the unions. Teach by example. Forget your own self and remember the sacred cause.
8. Aim at one goal - socialism.
9. Remember that the first steps toward this goal are: organization, education and self-education, daily united struggle for existence and for the conquest of state power.
10. Strive consciously for the emancipation of all people.

The characteristics of revolutionary activities of social-democrats listed above indicate a frame of mind of Party propagandists, who were transforming the class-consciousness within the revolutionary movement. V.I. Lenin described the results of the 1905 Revolution in a brief phrase: " After December they were no longer the same people. They had been reborn." (1) V.I. Lenin was in fact an ideal embodiment of the personality of the proletarian Revolution. In commemoration of Lenin's centenary the Central Committee of the CPSU stated, that: " Lenin was a political leader of a new type, a scholar, tribune and propagandist, an organizer of the masses. He was distinguished for his profound scientific approach in the analysis of events, sober assessment of the correlation and alignment of class forces, consistency and firmness in upholding Marxist principles, purposefulness in action, flexibility of tactics in the struggle, and selfless service to the interests and aims of the proletarian movement... a powerful intellect, an indomitable will, passionate hatred of slavery and oppression, revolutionary fervor, consistent internationalism, and boundless faith in the creative powers of the masses." (2)

A draft on Party Ethics, proposed by the Presidium of the Central Control Commission of the RCP(B) to a plenary meeting in 1924, states that in the current circumstances the part played by communists in the moral education of the masses should be enhanced. The difficulties of the country's internal life and the international situation, the draft states, compel us " to work out norms of comradship among its (Party) members, relationships between ourselves, norms of conduct towards the non-Party worker and peasant masses that will attract to communism the maximum number of new forces from the worker and peasant masses, ensure maximum confidence in us as the progressive revolutionary vanguard of the working class, and facilitate the transition to the new system."

The moral qualities of revolutionaries and personality characteristics of communists listed below were incorporated later in the Moral Code of the Builder of Communism. The negative personality traits should be eliminated and consciously erased from the mind of the working class:

1. He is not a Communist for whom the Party is not an aim but a means, who enters the Party in order to use his Party membership to obtain all kinds of privileges and advantages.
2. He is not a Communist who does something against which the Party is fighting.
3. He is not a Communist for whom the Party does not come first, but who gives the place to something else - his own household, family;
4. Therefore, the Communists must think not only of his work, but also of how to give others the opportunity of carrying

on this work as well;

5. The same attitude must be expected to the field of family relations. In present circumstances the communist family should be a group which, relying on natural feelings of attachment, seeks to create favorable conditions for the communist work of all members of the family, making it into a working comradely commune.

R E F E R E N C E S

1. V.I. Lenin, Collected Works, Vol. 28, p. 373. Institute of Marxism-Leninism, Moscow, Foreign Languages Publishing House, 1960-1970.
2. On the Centenary of the Birth of V.I. Lenin, Moscow, pp.4-5.

5. SOVIET TOTALITARIAN PERSONALITY

In her study, Soviet Political Indoctrination, Gayle Durham Hollander compiled various totalitarian personality concepts:

1. A lover of labor, a willing and enthusiastic contributor to the material growth of the Soviet economy.
2. Continual subjection of the individual will to that of the Party's leadership at any given time. Subordination of all personal emotions, needs, values, comforts, and interests to centrally determined goals.
3. Uncritical and enthusiastic acceptance of all Party pronouncements and orders.
4. Vigilance against not only one's inner enemies, the emotions, but also against other enemies.
5. A conscious sense of solidarity with workers in other countries.
6. Patriotic.
7. Collectivist, anti-individualistic, anti-egoist.
8. The virtues listed in the Moral Code of the Builder of

Communism (1961) are: humanism and mutual respect between people; honesty and truthfulness; moral purity and modesty in public and private life. Mutual respect in the family and concern for the upbringing of children; intolerance towards injustice, parasitism, careerism, and money-grabbing.
9. Atheistic, having no need for religion of any kind. (1)

The traditional Soviet personality models are based on the ideological principles of the Communist Party during the Lenin, Stalin and Khrushchev eras. These personality characteristics maintain their strong hold until the 23rd Party Congress of the CPSU; thereafter L. Brezhnev introduced the new directions for the Soviet social sciences. The new policy orientations of the social sciences prompted a chain of experimental research, especially within sociology and other related scientific fields, which evaluate value transformations and ideological re-assessments. Personality characteristics of the traditional image of Soviet man reflect a totalitarian value orientation. The glorification of the Party's leadership and the uncritical and enthusiastic acceptance of all Party orders by individual citizens has been correctly pointed out by American scholars of Soviet affairs during the past decades. (See summary of Western interpretations of Soviet personality characteristics).

Patriotism, vigilance, atheism, collectivism on the other hand, are slogans and propagandistic political concepts which have been used by Mao Tse-tung in the early period of the existence of the People's Republic of China and which, to some degree, still exist among the ideological and political guidelines of the Chinese Communist Party. Such Chinese personality values have been directly adopted from Stalinist ideological concepts and transplanted into the Chinese Communist mass-campaign, re-education, and remoulding campaigns.

R E F E R E N C E S

1. Gayle Durham Hollander, Soviet Political Indoctrination. Developments in Mass Media and Propaganda since Stalin. Praeger Special Studies, New York, 1975, pp.8-9.

6. PSYCHOLOGY OF THE SOVIET PERSONALITY

The traditional Russian experimental psychology, which studied detached processes and functions, was unable to find the proper way to study pedagogical phenomena. Psychological research after the October Revolution bears the imprint of a new Soviet psychology struggling with the idealist psychology which dominated, in the pre-revolutionary period, as the official science. " During the 1920's, Soviet psychology was still searching for the construction of psychology based on Marxist philosophy. Therefore, Soviet psychologists relied in many aspects on the research of foreign scholars. Research on the child's personality did not occupy a prominent position, and the psychology of child development was unable to penetrate the process of forming either the child's inner world or his behavior."(1)

Soviet psychologists have promoted the view that habits have decisive significance in the moral structure of the child's personality. (A.S. Makarenko, A.A. Smirnov, S.L. Rubinshteyn). The first to subject this problem to special psychological study was A.L. Shnirman, O nekotorykh voprosakh vospitaniya privychek. In: Sov. ped., 1941, No. 6, who showed that the formation of moral habits is a complex process of mastering appropriate forms of behavior; he also looked at their role in forming the moral qualities of the school aged child's personality. As a result of these investigations, the proposition was advanced that qualities or properties of personality are basically forms of child's social behavior fixed and stabilized by habits. It was determined that these forms of behavior, and by creating in the child a need to act in accordance with them, only takes place when their assimilation is accomplished by the child under the influence of his own motivation. Thus, the presence of a moral ideal in the child becomes a constantly acting motive which stimulates his behavior and activity, determines his values, the schema of his relation to reality. It is thereby the most important factor in the moral formation of the child's personality.

In recent years, in the Institute of Psychology of the USSR Academy of Pedagogical Sciences under the direction of L.I. Bozhovich, and in the Hertzen Leningrad State Pedagogical Institute under the direction of T.Ye. Konnikov, research has been undertaken on the directional development of the school-aged child personality and the role of the collective in forming this trend. The personality trend is here understood as a stable domination of the various motives for behavior, which subordinates all other motives and creates a definite structure in the motivational sphere. The most profound and fundamental characteristic of the personality is the trend in the area of human relations. The definite moral aspect of the personality is therefore directed towards those motives which dominate man: motives connected with self-centered egoistic interests or with interests with other people, or with social interests.

In the early 1950's the formation of different character traits was analyzed within the psychology of the Soviet personality, as for example, susceptibility to discipline, endurance, self-control, self-confidence, self-discipline, and sense of responsibility. Research has been undertaken on the growth of moral understanding, and on honor as a motive of conduct. A.G. Kovalev and V.I. Selivanov have written doctoral theses on the development of volitional personality traits; studies of the role of society in the formation of personality have continued. But the Soviet psychologists had not yet reached a decisive turning point at that time in the study of personality, especially with regard to the formation of the character and moral qualities of Soviet man."A.N. Leontiev's researches on the formation of man's psychic properties and processes, though positive, are only partly related to this problem; he has shown the conditioned-reflex nature of the system of connection underlying several elementary abilities, especially aural functions, and has advanced several important hypotheses relating to the systematic formation of psychic functions."(2)

Isolated studies have been confined to outlining what it is that is formed under the influence of the collective without elucidating how personality is formed, what are the forms of social influence, and how the collective itself develops. However, the process of formation of permanent human qualities has been made by L.I. Bozhovich.

The ideological and political atmosphere in the Soviet Union presupposed that psychologists could not add anything significant to what the classics of Marxism had already contributed about personality. Until the 1950's Soviet publications on personality were geared along these lines, and both the study of personality and of social psychology were poor. Since the 1950's, significant changes occured as a greater awareness of the need to understand the individual personality developed. The topic of social psychology was discussed for the first time in 1965. However, there is a growing tendency today in the Soviet Union to by-pass the statement of purely theoretical positions to a more concrete and pertinent analysis. Soviet social scientists must have concluded that there is a need for the development of a system of concepts which would be able to express man's integrated behavior. K.K. Platonov describes four groups of personality characteristics:

1. " Socially determined characteristics, especially man's purposefulness and moral qualities. The Substructure of the personality includes personal interests, aspirations, and ideals of the personality. It further includes the individual world view of the personality, as well as its moral and political views. Furthermore, the relationship towards one self, towards other people and towards work.
2. Biologically determined characteristics such as temperament, instincts and elementary needs: The second substructure called " experience ", defines the skills and education of the personality. These various concepts of different personality formations are intervowen and integrated in the various substructures. For example, the knowledge of moral norms from this substructure are the basis of the moral views from the first substructure.
3. The third substructure of the personality appears as individual characteristics of different psychological processes. Such psychological processes appear in its essence as a reflection of the real world. Based on the teachings of I.P. Pavlov, we have to distinguish the forms of first-signals: emotions and feelings, and second signals, the thinking process, perception, feelings and the will-power.
4. The fourth substructure of the personality appears as a basis of biological qualities which we call temper or the typological characteristics of the personality, as B.M. Teplov defines it." (3)

" Soviet psychologists have been particularly attracted to the problem of the relationship between characteristics of the nervous activity and features of personality, notably temperamental qualities, character traits and aptitudes. Teplov, 1961, Nebylitsin, 1969, Ilina, 1963, Kopytova, 1964."

Merlin, in his analysis of the personality, distinguishes between general and individual characteristics. He distinguishes between the personality characteristics, which are of a social nature, and between individual characteristics. The first category includes the individual's position towards other people, work, science, art, individual and social property, as well as toward himself. Their social nature consists in their being ultimately a product of social ideology and social psychology.

" Soviet psychologists and philosophers have been critical of the view that certain developments in human society, like industrialization or automation, result in the appearance in certain feelings, notably that of alienation. They further argue that socialism has resulted in a maximum development of the personality and, implicitly, in the greatest decrease in feelings of alienation. (Krylov, 1964, Bueva, 1965) " (5)

Soviet psychologists have made a strong plea for the concrete study of individual personality. Many writers urge a move away trom abstract formulations which were merely s restatement of the principle of dialectical materialism applied to society and the individual. Such views appear as opposing the dogma that only class psychology exists. (Kovalev, 1963, Kozyrev, 1965, Ramul, 1965). Selivanov wrote in this connection: " All Soviet psychologists mean by personality, not a man in general, but a concrete individual, a member of a certain society who has complex relationships to the other people. Such a concept of personality requires that the study be particularly concrete, in order to reflect the diversity of human life... It is necessary to penetrate deeper into the Soviet man's life, to know his activity, behavior, mind as they are in reality. " (6).

R E F E R E N C E S

1. L.I. Bozhovich, L.S. Slavina, Fifty Years of Soviet Psychology of Upbringing. In: Voprosy psikhologii, 1967, 13 (5). pp. 51-70. In: Psychology in the USSR: A Historical Perspective. Ed., J. Brozek, and D.I. Slobin, International Arts and Sciences Press, Inc., White Plains, New York, 1968.
2. A.N. Leontiev, The Nature and Formation of Human Psychic Properties. p. 226.
3. K.K. Platonov, Sotsial'noe i biologicheskoe v strukture lichnosti.
4. Levy Rahmani, Soviet Psychology. N.Y. 1973, p. 349.

5. Levy Rahmani, p. 350.
6. Selivanov, On the Concrete Study of the Personality of Soviet Man. Ed., E.I. Ignatev. In: Problems of the Psychology of the Personality, p. 38.

7. CURRENT SOVIET RESEARCH ON PERSONALITY

The current typologies of Soviet personality have in addition to political and ideological concepts also different scientific-theoretical grounds - neurophysiological, psychophysiological, psychological, sociophysiological, and sociological. Different concepts that are not in sufficient agreement with each other claim to be the integrating personality principle, such as the concept of the ' direction of the personality ' developed by D.U. Uznadze, and the concept of ' relations ' by V.N. Myasishchev. Psychologists who study personality usually narrow their task, defining the nucleus of the personality as the subject of conscious activity in the sphere of motivation, and isolate within its needs and tendencies. Progress has been made in recent years in evaluating self-consciousness, the capacities for self-evaluation and self-respect, on which the level of aspirations and real behavior largely depend, which is important for the normal functiong of the personality (V.S. Merlin). In recent years, new results have been achieved in differential psychology and differential psycho-physiology (B.M. Teplov), which studies the differences between individuals.

However, the formation of a unified Soviet personality structure represents a complex problem within Soviet psychology. The personality is seen by Soviet psychologists as the apex of the mental process of man, since it represents the highest level of self-orientation and self-guidance. Reynval'd defined a self-directed personality into three factors:

1. " The realization of one self as a subject of specific activities.
2. The ability to adopt environmental influences and to transform one self within such environments, specifically the

volitional transformation of the personality.
3. The adaptation of desirable qualities and the elimination of undesirable characteristics."(1)

A further aspect of the psychology of the Soviet personality deals with the concept of the will in relationship to personality formation and behavior modification. The will of man forms a higher level of self-regulation and gives man the choice of free behavior and the intellectual ability to control his life. " Soviet psychology views the will of man as a specific human reflection of brain activities, which is seen as a precondition of conscious regulation of man over his behavior."(2) The will is related to intelligence and emotions, as pointed out by I.M. Sechenov: " The will is not any kind of impersonal agent; it is the active part of the mind and moral emotions; it regulates such activities in the name of self-preservation."(3)

The volitional qualities of the personality are the creation of original capabilities of man solving obstacles during the realization of goals. The volitional qualities are related to premediated actions. Man can regulate his conscious activities with the assistance of volitional qualities. Therefore, we have to distinguish between two aspects of volitional qualities of the personality:

1. The motivation of the personality and its corresponding goals.
2. The behavioral characteristics of the personality, which accomplish such goals.

" Motivation of the personality, or the direction of the personality, form the concept of the will of man."(4) Further personality types within Soviet psychology include a progressive personality and an ideological personality. A progressive personality is a personality which contains emotions of personal responsibility for progress - that is, a socially active personality. The ideological personality is a personality which accomplishes a maximum development of individual capabilities in connection with social change and in overcoming alienation and self-estrangement. The dialectics of personality is seen within Soviet psychology in this relationship:

1. The single personality in relationship towards a mass personality.
2. The struggle between individualism and the formation of a unique personality.

Social feelings of man communicate social values within the society. Feelings relate man to man and man to society. The value of man's existence is not why he exists, how he relates to the exterior world and to other people, and how he satisfies his desires. " The personality is formed by how and to what degree and with what kind of social experience man is able to master difficulties of life."(5)

V.G. Anan'yev analyzed the human being as an open and closed system and illustrated the inner relationship of these qualities. " In such a closed system of human existence we find an open relationship with the world, where relationships between tendencies and potentials of man are formed, the self-realization of the ' I ' - the core of the human personality."(6) An independent personality is preconditioned by the inner developmental process of social-political activities, self-consciousness, social status, professional position, social functions, personal value orientations, and the personality structure as a whole. Soviet social psychology coined the term " the psychological hope of man ", which includes the ability of man to be himself, to experience his " I ", and to develop his individuality under different conditions. " Permanency and steadiness form the autonomy of the personality. The central value center of human existence is connected with the personality structure. This center determines the values of life and its self-conduct. Within the Marxist theory, the value orientation has the regulatory function of the personality with regard to social values."(7)

Intellectual activity underlines the fact that personality cannot be reduced to its expression in the form of activity alone; harmony between personality and activity is possible only by endowing activity with human meaning. Otherwise, a purely instrumental interpretation of man as merely a tool for the activity which is over and above him is unavoidable; this serves as an ideological precondition for the totalitarian organization of social life.

The formation process of the personality within Soviet psychology further parallels the development of the will. Activities without the participation of the will are non-personal and non-personality oriented. " However, the will is not the beginning and also not the core of the personality. The will is an important part of the personality structure. The personality is structured by various aspects of activities of the subject, which originates its developmental process of human relations within a social environment."(8)

a. Sociology and Soviet Personality

The Marxist-Leninist concepts of the personality structure have been analyzed from different aspects by the following contemporary Soviet sociologists and philosophers: E.A.Anufriev, L.M. Arkhangel'skiy, V.G. Afanas'yev, V.G. Bueva, L.P. Voytko, V.I. Gak, G.M. Glezerman, G.E. Ivanov, I.S. Myslivchenko, A.T. Ostryanin, D.F. Smirnov, G.L. Sokhan', L.V. Tugarinov, V.P. Kharchev, A.G. Shinkaruk, V.I. Shishkin, A.F. Yakuby, and others.

Marxist sociology of the personality does research on many different levels, including changes in the social type of the personality and its degree of freedom as a function of the character of the social order, the correlation among autonomous factors in the socialization of the personality in different social systems, and the personality in the organization. It also investigates the principle governing the social interaction of individuals in different social groups and needs, motives, and value orientations of the personality that regulate social behavior.

The study of the social system makes it possible to understand the value orientations of the personality, its aspirations and ideological orientations and the possible degree of its creative manifestations. But social behavior is determined not only by a person's present standing, but also by his past experience and by the character of the cultural values that he has assimilated. Each individual, as a personality, is a product not only of existing relations, but also of all previous history. The ideal of Marxist humanism is not to dissolve the personality in an impersonal " mass ", but harmoniously to combine the personal and the social. I.S. Kon explains the term personality in connection with sociological analysis, as"characterizing the social peculiarities of individuals as a sum of integrated social values. Social values are formed as an integral part of human relations; they transform man into a subject of labor, cognition and socialization." (9)

A number of intricate social problems such as the dialectic of the development of the personality and the social division of labor, ways of converting labor into the primary vital necessity of the personality, and the correlation between subjective activity and inter-personal contacts, arise in connection with such a concept. The development of creative activity of each individual, which is inseparably connected with a sense of social and moral responsibility, is the most important prerequisite for the shaping of the new man and new personality within Soviet sociology.

b. Soviet Social Psychology and Personality Changes

Within the past 10 years, there has been a dynamic development of social psychology in the USSR, notably evaluating habits, customs, and traditional values within the society. Other psychological aspects, such as emotions and social relations have not been sufficiently considered in connection with the formation of human values. " Soviet psychology developed the aspects of emotionality and human feelings only after the traditional values of human existence were established."(10)

Contemporary social-psychological concepts of the Soviet personality and mentality are expressed through the social dynamics of labor relations. Subjective factors of personality development and the educative role of communist principles are part of the formation process of the Soviet social psychology. The ideological development in the USSR has a strong impact on the relationship between the personality structure and the social-psychological development of the human value system. The ideological basis for communist social psychology is the scientific world outlook, which claims that a human being is not free in the Soviet society until he has been able to develop all potentials of his personality which will serve the whole society. Man is free only when he has been able to develop his spiritual powers and his social consciousness, which appear as inner-personal necessity.

The humanization of existence is formed by satisfying human spiritual and creative needs, which are present in every human being. The necessities of inner-spiritual values of human existence are characterized by:

1. " The desire for free and creative enjoyment of work;
2. The desire for cognition and the spiritual assimilation of the world; the scientific, philosophical and aesthetic search of beauty.
3. The desire for a behavior model which will embrace all people in their search for truthful human morality.
4. The desire for emotional enrichment and the satisfaction of aesthetic needs; a deep love between man and wife, and between parent and child; finally, an emotional relationship between all people."(11)

The humanization of man's existence enriches his consciousness and expands the dimensions of his mind; in addition, it also enriches his emotions. However, different kinds of emotions develop within the Soviet society. " Emotions of collectivity, emotions of comradeship,emotions of patriotism, emotions of internationalism, optimism, cheerfulness and passion." (12) In accordance with the development of the human mind, emotions appear as the creative-spiritual ability of the personality which compliment material and spiritual values of life. The spiritual enrichment of man is a developmental process of necessities and social interchange of people. Both are guided by moral principles. Specific characteristics and objective regularities of communist progress are the consciously and systematically structured character of man. The systematic character of progress is the social achievement of socialism which accelerates human activities."The spiritual richness of the communist personality forms a communist belief system. The belief system is the pivot of the whole psychological structure of man. The communist belief as a personality characteristic of the new man began its formation process at the same time as the proletarian personality structure was formed."(13) The level of communist belief is unequally distributed among Soviet people, since the progressive elements of communism include: " The psychological structure of the personality, its political spectrum, the social-economic and moral consciousness, the emotional and willpower structure of the Soviet people."(14) One finds, in Soviet society, people with different character variations and communist value perceptions. One category of people is characterized by strict obedience to the principles of communism with regard to their social relations, which, on the other hand, are not able to keep pace with the development of political consciousness and communist needs. Another category of people is characterized by the discrepancy between human ideals and the conduct of the people.

The Soviet personality structure and the dynamics of personality formation have, in many ways, a conservative developmental tendency. The personal value of people is often determined by their emotional stability. Emotions and feelings, in comparison with general psychological concepts, have their specific regularities, which are not part of every personality structure and which are not visible in every situation of life and are not controlled by the will. In situations of life, emotionality prevails and hinders the development of intellectual capabilities of the personality, weakening, at the same time, its willpower. Such personality development dictates the behavioral attitudes, which are contrary to the best interests of the Soviet society and are also in contradiction to individual personalities. " This, however, means, that man is incapable of controlling his own feelings and his own life. Those individuals do not have the opportunity and the power to overcome the duality between consciousness and emotions, and willpower on the other. The elimination of the conflict situation is seen in the participation of workers collectives." (15)

R E F E R E N C E S

1. N.I. Reynval'd, Lichnost' kak predmet psikhologicheskogo analiza. Izdatel'skoe ob'edinenie " Visha Shkola ". Izdatel'stvo pri Kharkovskom gosudarstvennom universitete, Kharkov, 1974, p. 155.

2. K.K. Platonov, Ed., Lichnost' i trud. Izdatel'stvo " Mysl' ", Moskva, 1965, p. 180.

3. I.M. Sechenov, Izbrannye proizvedeniya. Tom I. p. 255.

4. Ibid. p. 181.

5. V.V. Korshunova, Dialekticheskoe edinstvo individual'no psikhologicheskikh osobenostey i obshchestvennykh chert lichnosti. Izdatel'stvo L'vovskogo universiteta, 1967.

6. A.G. Anan'yev, Chelovek kak predmet poznaniya. P. 328.

7. Tu.V. Sychev, Mikrosreda i lichnost'. Filosofskie i sotsiologicheskie aspekty. Izdatel'stvo " Mysl' ", Moskva, 1974, p. 131.

8. Leont'yev, A.N., Deyatel'nost' i lichnost'. Voprosy Filosofii, 1974, No. 4 and 5.

9. I.S. Kon, Sotsiologiya lichnosti. Moskva, 1967, p. 7.

10. Stroitel'stvo kommunizma i dukhovnyy mir cheloveka. Izdatel'stvo " Nauka ", Moskva, 1966, p. 105.

11. Yu.N. Semenov, Obshchestvennyy progress i sotsial'naya filosofiya sovremennoy burzhuazii.

12. L.V. Sokhan', Dukhovnyy progress lichnosti i kommunizm. Akademiya Nauk Ukrainskoy SSR, Institut Filosofii, Kiev, Naukova Dumka, 1966, p. 228.

13. Ibid. p. 223.

14. Ibid. p. 223.

15. Ibid. p. 231.

B. THEORETICAL CONCEPTS OF THE SOVIET PERSONALITY

1. THE POLITICAL AND IDEOLOGICAL GUIDELINES OF DESIRED SOVIET PERSONALITY MODELS

The formation of a new personality structure within the Soviet social sciences has great significance and political importance for the development of the human value system and philosophical world view of the USSR. The structure of the contemporary Soviet personality changes social relations within the society, as well as the general conditions of existence. The concept of the personality is defined by its direct involvement in social action. " Only those can become individuals and personalities who possess original qualities-depth of feeling, originality of thought. Every person is an individual, a personality, by virtue of the fact that he possesses certain socially significant features." (1) The concept of personality is further described as " a concrete expression of the essence of man, i.e., the integration in a given individual of socially significant features related to the essence of the given society." (2)

The basic question, however, was what kind of personality was to be produced, with what qualities, aspirations, and ideals. It was answered by V.I. Lenin in the briefest possible way: " Learn communism." (3) Characterizing the importance of the collective and group mentality, Maxim Gorky wrote, " The collective creates a person of a completely different kind of mentality, more active, more steadfast, more able to act, and the will to build life from the will of the whole collective." (4) " The formation of the new Soviet personality is the result of educational work. The character of the Soviet man was forged, the character of a fighter, revolutionary and conscious working man." (5)

The personality of the Soviet man, states the Program of the CPSU, is effected by the participation in communist construction and the development of communist principles in the economic and social spheres, under the influence of education which is carried out by the Party and various social organizations. The development of a well-rounded personality is a long and complex process, depending on material and cultural circumstances and on the depth and scope of ideological participation. The comprehension of these problems, the search for new ways of dealing with them, the elaboration of new forms and methods of education and continuous persistent efforts to put into practice the ideals of communism constitute the main substance of the diverse activities of the Soviet Communist Party in educating members of the entire society. To characterize the new personality that is shaping the whole Soviet society, one must reveal the fundamental changes in the areas of social relations, productivity, social activity, and mutual relationships between people and society. " The degree of development of the personality in society cannot be defined by characterizing the qualities of separate individuals or even groups of individuals. It is determined by the content, the intensity of relations between all groups, all sections of society. The transformation of the personality under socialism has expressed itself in the development of the scientific world view."(6)

Through the systematic research on personal and intellectual value orientations, the Soviet Communist Party leadership becomes directly involved in shaping the personal values of Soviet citizens. Research on personality development in the USSR is directed towards a functioning attitude of individual creativity, individual self-consciousness and individual autonomy. " It is known that the problems of motivation and social relationships are extremely difficult and are particularly susceptible to the errors of idealism. When one has to rebuild a science from its very foundations, it is unwise to tackle first the problem that is most difficult and most likely to lead astray. In our efforts to escape the dangers of idealism, we fell into the error of extreme mechanism."(7) The goal of developing a new aspect of contemporary Soviet psychology of personality lies in ' desirable behavior ', or ' practical importance ', which can be further used, manipulated, oriented, and motivated. The present Soviet human value system survives only in individual and collective motivation, and political activism in connection with developing and applying the principles of the scientific-technological revolution.

Man is the central problem of Marxist-Leninist philosophy, psychology, sociology, law, biology, medicine and art. The teaching about man forms the methodological basis for the solution of many theoretical problems and practical tasks in building a communist society. Questions about personality development are quite visible in Lenin's thinking. Once, during the October Revolution, Lenin was asked, " What will be the most difficult problem to be faced in building socialism and communism?" He pondered for a moment and answered, ' The moulding of the New Man.' " (8)

a. The Ideal Image of the Soviet Worker's Personality

The world view of the Soviet personality centers on personal beliefs. Moral stability and personal beliefs of Soviet workers are best described in Table I., where answers to the questions " What is your ideal of man? What do you most value in people?" are categorized. The responses characterize an individual who, is for the majority of the population, an ideal person. Such an individual is politically conscious, honest, and a work-loving human being, cultivated, with a strong drive for dignity. The percentage of workers giving priority to the first answer (68%) is the result of how the question was formulated. Ideological and moral qualities have been combined in one question. The ideological concept of human values would have gotten a much lower percentage of answers if asked separately. This is also evident in answers given to questions No. 3 and No. 4. In answer No.3 culture is combined with interpersonal relations; in answer No. 4 dishonesty and insincerity are objected by 42% of the responses. Ideological qualities, as related to personality characteristics of workers, would receive, therefore, not more than 26% of affirmative answers, if we deduct the percentage of answers of No. 4 from No. 1.

Table I.

WHAT DO YOU MOST VALUE IN PEOPLE? WHAT IS YOUR IDEAL OF MAN?*

1. Ideological and moral qualities: intelligence, honesty, justice	68
2. Conscientious and disciplined at work	30
3. Human culture, attentive relationship among people	55
4. Don't like: dishonesty, insincerity, hypocrisy, lack of discipline, drunkeness	42

* K.K. Platonov, Ed., Lichnost' i trud. Izdatel'stvo " Mysl'", Moskva, 1965, p. 234.

Contemporary Soviet society is structured and subdivided into ideal and progressive personality groups. Therefore, we have to determine, what a progressive personality is, and when specific objectives of such a progress are found. A.I. Tatarenko provides the definition of a progressive personality, which is divided into various developmental stages of human values.

1. " To deepen man's knowledge about nature, society and himself.
2. The realization of man's existence and the interpretations of his social obligations; the realization of a strong consciousness and self-consciousness.
3. To expand the spiritual freedom of the personality; to free the personality from religious and idealistic influences and to change man's goals in life.
4. To improve the concept of human feelings and emotions.
5. To develop spiritual and creative qualities of the personality and to increase its activity within the material and spiritual perception of reality."(9)

The description of the physical perfection and the image of man in connection with personality development of the progressive and contemporary Soviet citizen is given by Mikhaylov. The perfect physical image of man has:

1. " Good health.
2. The development of physical qualities in connection with moral and will-power qualities, with emphasis on positive habits and a maximum functioning of the human organism.
3. The adaptation of special working procedures which enable the individual to be highly productive in both, physical and spiritual performance.
4. A harmonious development of the human body and a balanced coordination of its functions."(10)

D.D. Ryabov described the progressive Soviet personality as formed with the following human and professional qualifications and values:

1. " A high degree of scientific and professional knowledge, political maturity, and profound perception of cultural values.
2. A cultivated taste for aesthetic values; the adoption of

contemporary production methods, devotion to the principles of communism and a deep love for the socialist motherland, as well as for other socialist countries.
3. A conscientious worker for the well being of the whole society. Protection of common property; conscientious performance of social duties with regard to the protection of social interests.
4. Collectivism and fraternal assistance; respect for other human beings; integrity and truthfulness, simplicity and modesty in social and private life.
5. Mutual respect within the family, care for the education of children; irreconcilability with injustice, parasitism, dishonesty, greediness and careerism.
6. No tolerance of national or racial discrimination. Fraternal solidarity with workers of all nations."(11)

The characteristics of the contemporary Soviet personality traits have been succinctly described and interpreted by A.I. Tatarenko, V. Mikhaylov, and D.D. Ryabov. Major developmental trends of the Soviet personality structure are characterized by 1. A progressive personality. 2. Physical perfection in addition to specific personality traits. 3. A professional personality structure, which is oriented towards cultural and scientific-technological accomplishments. Subdivisions of the above personality concepts will be analyzed in separate chapters.

R E F E R E N C E S

1. Georgi Smirnov, The Soviet Man. Progress Publishers, Moscow, 1973, p. 45.
2. Sotsiologiya v SSSR, Redaktor G.V. Osipov, Moskva, "Mysl' ", 1965, 2 v. p. 492.
3. V.I. Lenin, Collected Works, Vol. 28, p. 408.
4. Maxim Gorky, Collected Works, Vol. 17, p. 193.
5. 50th Anniversary of the Great October Socialist Revolution, Moscow, 1967, p. 46.
6. Georgi Smirnov, p. 300.
7. Y. Bronfenbrenner, Some Views of Soviet Psychology. American Psychological Ass. Washington, D.C. 1962, p. 66.
8. Fyodor Konstantinov, The Moulding of a Harmoniously Developed Individual. In: SOCIAL SCIENCES, Vol. 7, No.4, 1976, p. 43.

9. A.I. Tatarenko, Kriteriy nravstvennogo progressa. Moskva, " Mysl' ", 1967, p. 157.
10. V. Mikhaylov, Fizicheskaya kul'tura v period stroitel'stva kommunizma. Moskva, Fizkul'tura i sport, 1964, p. 21.
11. D.D. Ryabov, Sotsialisticheskoe gosudarstvo i vospitanie novogo cheloveka. Izdatel'stvo Moskovskogo universiteta, 1972, p. 32.

2. SOVIET LITERATURE AND PERSONALITY FORMATION

Socialist realism is the aesthetic value system of contemporary Soviet art, named after the dominant artistic style. Socialist realism has as its artistic goal a method that allows writers to depict life in its continous movement and historical development, and organically to blend the most sober realism with the most profound socialist ideological content, high artistry with clear understanding of historical meaning.

"... Socialist literature is literature that has undergone the influence of ideas of the construction of socialism. The most diverse shades of the socialist world view find expression in it. However, various conflicting artistic tendencies, different methods of work, are possible in socialist literature, since sympathy for socialism is the only precondition for the elaboration of a new aesthetic world view. Socialist realism arises in the depths of socialist literature as an inalienable part of the latter. But it is not just a part, it is the vanguard..."(1)

The problem of socialist art does not abolish the problem of socialist realism as a new direction in the artistic development and as a creative method. Socialist realism, as the aesthetic expression of the new Soviet society, as a creative method of the contemporary literature arises at a definite historical stage in the development of value systems, in the development of art in general, socialist art in particular. Socialist realism dates back to the day of the birth of the historically new man; it is formed in the process of the internal development of literature as such. M. Gorky formulated and defined socialist realism as a " realistic, imaginative thought based on socialist experience."(2)

The Soviet Communist Party's approach to literature is strictly utilitarian: good literature is that which promotes government policies and educates the masses in the spirit of communism. This has been the Party's position right from the start. In an article written in 1905, " Party Organization and Party Literature," V.I. Lenin wrote:

" Literature must become party literature. In contrast to the bourgeois practices... the bourgeois businessman's approach to literature... with its career-seeking and individualism... socialist proletariat must put forward the principle of party literature and try to implement this principle in actual practice as thoroughly and as completely as possible."(3)

Lenin's advice was followed literally, and all the resolutions adopted at the subsequent party congresses echoed his concern for the creation of party literature. The official proclamation on Socialist Realism as the approved method for Soviet literature was made in 1934 at the First Congress of Soviet writers.

J.V. Stalin followed the direction of party literature and formed his own concept of proletarian literature. " ...truthfulness and historical concreteness of artistic depiction must be combined with the task of ideological remoulding and re-education of the toiling people in the spirit of Socialism. This method in fiction and in literary criticism is what we call Socialist Realism... To be an engineer of human souls means to stand with both feet firmly planted on the ground in real life. This, in turn, means breaking away from old-type romanticism, from that romanticism which depicted non-existent life and non-existent characters, diverting the reader from the contradictions of life into a world of impossible, a world of Utopia." (4)

a. Theoretical Concept of the Soviet ' Personality of Art '

Many Soviet writers and artists are undertaking a process of remoulding people and forming personality values with communist characteristics. " The transformation process is conducted under conditions of an ideological struggle which embraces many aspects of daily life and in fact represents a battle for the mind and heart of the people. The major obstacle in such a battle, however, are the centuries of traditional values and beliefs of the Russian people."(5)

The goals established for the Soviet writers and artists were made clear by the official statement of N.S. Khrushchev at the 21st Party Congress of the CPSU. ..." to show our people not only as they are today, but to peep into their tomorrow, to help to illuminate the road ahead with a searchlight - such is the task of every conscious Soviet writer. ... While selecting the best sentiments and qualities of Soviet man, disclosing to him his tomorrow, we must at the same time, show our people what they must not be, we must scourge the vestiges of yesterday, which prevent Soviet people from marching forward."

Aesthetics has the obligation to reunite the theoretical and historical aspect of the ' art of personality '. Kagan, in his writings on art theories, considers folk art, traditional architecture and sculpture as nationalistic art, since they are not directly related to the creativity of an individual personality. The historical process increased the role of the personality by creating artistic values which did not separate the artist from social environment. The dialectic-materialistic concept of the personality and society is the social image of the personality; it is expressed through the personality of the artist. The artist communicates through artistic creativity the world outlook of different societies, groups, classes and nations; it is only then, that a society is able to accept the aesthetic values of the self-image of the personality in relationship to ideological and aesthetic values of a collective. Kagan says further that... " the activity of the personality within artistic creativity changes during different social-historical developments and with regard to different artistic styles. We distinguish between creativity and assiduity: In the first instance, the personality characteristics are present in the idea of creative concepts of the artist. In the second instance, the personality appears in the selection of the performing dramatic and musical work of art, as well as in the ideological and aesthetic interpretation of the original artwork. The second aspect can also be analyzed by comparing the individual and collective aspects of creativity; the concept of the collective personality differs from the individual personality concept in artistic creativity; each member of the collective process in theatre, film, music, has to be attuned with the activities of all members of the collective.

An additional aspect of artistic creativity is preconditioned not by skill and talent and the ideological orientation of the artist, but by his perception of the world, by the richness of his soul, by the intensity of his feelings, the integrity of his nature, the nobility and eminence of his creative aspirations, the richness of his performance (poetry, lyrics, epics)." (6) Kagan relates the personality concept to artistic creativity in saying that the personality as a subject of creative activities questions the performance of the personality of artists within art history; that the personality is an object of artistic figurative cognition; and that personality as a subject of artistic perception includes the formation process of the personality and its aesthetic education.

The aesthetic development of the personality awakens many hidden talents of man; for example, the artistic-creative talents and a flexibility of the personality in applying those talents. The aesthetic development of the personality strengthens the intellectual ability of human beings and enriches their emotions; it further forms aesthetic ideals and intensifies the participation of human beings in every day life.

Aesthetic desires materialize through the productivity of labor. The aesthetic culture of the personality appears in the relationship between people and their productive orientation and within the purposefulness of being. Soviet man tries to respond to his needs for harmony and beauty, and not only to communist ethics. The spiritual process of the communist personality is a unification of ethical and aesthetic attitudes of the personality which relate to people and the environment.

The educational role of socialist art consists of educating not only the mind, but also human emotions. Its task is to mould man's political, moral and ideological notions as intellectual and emotional attitudes and as convictions and feelings. It is the aesthetic nature of art, which, above all, educates men through a model given to the public in an artistic form.

The dominant themes of Soviet art shape the character of

the new Soviet man. The depicted positive hero is a representative of the masses, who embodies the contemporary features of Soviet man, as Baluyev in Kozhevnikov's novel MEET BALUYEV, Krylov in Granin's INTO THE STORM, Bakhirev in Nikolayeva's BATTLE OF THE WAY, further the heros of the book by Remenchuk, the film POEM OF THE SEA, directed by Dovzhenko, Arbuzov's plays and the paintings of Salakhov.

Every culture and social system has its individual characteristics and value of man, even though not every society has a developed personality concept. " Therefore, the selection of characters in describing the personality in literature is associated with the developmental stage of social relations and the ideological orientation of particular writers." (7) From the cultural and historical perspective, the concept of the personality is seen as a creative form, as a carrier of material and spiritual values. Personality traits appear as creative stimuli which define the individual participation in cultural life. Therefore, the artist has to be interested in general, as well as in specific, peculiarities of the personality. The typology of such characteristics within a given culture has unique and non-repetitive values. Such an individual personality is in conformity with its inner and exterior, innate and cultural, physical and spiritual characteristics of human existence. The personality searches for specific information which is inevitable for its activity, for the accomplishments of its inner goals, for the reinforcement of inner ' vulnerable ' factors. The cognitive function of value-orientation directs the intellectual interests toward determined objects. The coordination of inner-psychological life, specifically the emotional and will-oriented aspects of the personality is a further step toward personality formation. The psychological processes have to be harmoniously attuned with one another; they have to coincide with the condition of the activity. The value orientations are formed with predetermined images of life. On the other hand, value orientations hinder the origin of the psychological condition, which disrupts the normal process of activity.

The structural level of the personality is subjective with regard to its emotional condition, its thinking attitudes and phantasies; it appears as an object,however, in its behavior and cultural expression. However, the subjective elements are not always communicated, and the objective elements of art are not always experienced. " Personal relations of artistic creativity reflect an existentialist experience. The childhood is a fundamental existentialist structure, the early adult years form some basic parts of life in connection with the formation of character. The adult years glorify the power of emotional richness and life experience."(8)

REFERENCES

1. " Oktyabr ", No. 6. 1967, p. 196.
2. Maxim Gorky, Collected Works, Vol. 27. p. 44.
3. Quoted in L. Timofeev, " Russkaya sovetskaya literatura. Moskva, 1952, p. 7.
4. G. Struve, Soviet Russian Literature, 1917-1950. University of Oklahoma Press, 1951, p. 245.
5. G.I. Lomidze, Ed., Novyy chelovek, Novyy gumanizm. Izdatel'-stvo " Mysl' ", Moskva, 1969, Akademiya obshchestvennykh Nauk pri TsK KPSS, p. 90.
6. M.S. Kagan, Iskusstvo i lichnost'. Voprosy Filosofii, 1967. No. 12. p. 129.
7. D.S. Likhachev, Chelovek v literatury drevney Rusi. Moskva, 1970.
8. E.V. Sokolov, Kul'tura i lichnost'. Akademiya Nauk SSSR, Institut Filosofii, Leningradskogo sektora; Izdatel'stvo " Nauka ", Leningradskoe otdelenie, Leningrad, 1972, p. 179.

3. COMMUNIST CONSCIOUSNESS AND PERSONALITY CHARACTERISTICS

Sociologists at Gor'ky University surveyed several hundred people by asking them: " How do you view life and labor in a communist society?" 85% answered - a high degree of consciousness and personal commitemnt; 65% said that work is the source of satisfaction; 70% said that the standard of living should be improved and consumers demands be met; 18% didn't know anything about communism or communist consciousness; 11% did not answer at all. (Table II.)

Table II.

HOW DO YOU VIEW LIFE AND LABOR IN A COMMUNIST SOCIETY?*

ANSWERS	% of answers in relationship to the number of questioned
1. People in a communist society schould have a highly developed consciousness and a personal commitment	85
2. Productive work is the source of personal satisfaction and important for the whole society	65
3. The standard of living should be improved and consumer's demands will be satisfied	70
4. Have vague views about communism	18
5. Did not answer	11

* K.K. Platonov, Ed., Lichnost' i trud. Izdatel'stvo "Mysl' ", Moskva, 1965, p. 230.

The high percentage of answers to the first question is the result of the formulation of the question; communist consciousness and personal commitment are combined; personal commitment would definitely receive a higher percentage of answers, if asked separately, since it does not have a political connotation and would appear simply as a question of general personality value. The third question is most important. 70% plead for a higher living standard and for meeting consumer demands. Those answers indicate the absence of basic means of normal living conditions within the particular area of the Soviet society. The high percentage of answers to the third question can also be interpreted as social criticism and a general dissatisfaction with the communist system itself. The answers to the fourth and fifth questions illustrate the indifference toward communist beliefs and consciousness and can be interpreted as anti-systemic. Those people could be placed among the passive oppositionists. The personality characteristics with reference to this survey study can be described and characterized as socially critical and anti-systemic.

The development of individual consciousness is characterized by ideas, beliefs, habits and guidelines which conform to communist ethics. Scientific communism examines the formation process of the new socialist type of personality. " During the period of transition to communism there is a possibility to educate a new man who harmoniously combines the spiritual richness, the moral purity and physical perfection of man."(1) The essence of man is the result of social relations and of man's activities during his life time. The theory of scientific communism provides a concrete analysis of the revolutionary transformation process of the intellectual capacity and spiritual creativity in exploring the interrelationship between objective and subjective factors of particular transformation processes. Kharchev defines the process of personality development during the transitional period from capitalism to communism as follows: " The development and education of man is a high communist ideal. Formation of the personality structure is twofold: It is formed outside the society and through the influence of the society. The formation of the personality is idetntified as a value formation of the ' social reproduction of man '."(2) Parygin emphasized that the structural characteristics of personality, as described in contemporary Soviet social psychology, do not hide the responsibilities of general psychological and social-psychological aspects of personality development and a conscious attitude of the personality toward society. Parygin further pointed out the importance of the formation process of the world outlook, the readiness to work and social participation of man should be analyzed only within psychology."(3) Tselikova described the formation process of the personality as well as the new type of Soviet man within the framework of philosophical-ethical value perception and conscious attitudes toward change."(4)

Marxist ethics considers the ethical self-perfection of the personality in relationship to its ethical development as an aspect in creating active and conscious human values. These values should be directed toward the elimination of human deficiencies and promote dignity which is defined as social morality. " The moral development of the personality demands a directed education, the development of moral goals of the personality related to the problems of the society."(5) The moral development of the personality further includes the self-development of the personality ("I" structure), its moral power, its moral persuasive ability, and its strong intention to further this value system which is a necessary precondition of moral development. Such a tendency of moral development relates to expectations of people. " The personality development is also asocial in relationship to the collective, if it does not fulfill the functions of production and if it contains a moral value system which is not in conformity with the interests of the collective."(6)

Sociological research indicates that major parts of moral development of the personality support the creative character of work within the Soviet Union, as well as its perspectives of professional improvement, especially within labor relations. The moral aspect of the personality is expressed in the perception of duty, communist consciousness, honor, human dignity and happiness, as it relates to self-confirmation in the society. " Moral ideas of the personality are based on ideological orientation, one's class consciousness and one's political views which are influenced by objective and subjective personality factors."(7)

The character of man is structured by different personality traits: 1. The definition of the personality; 2. The psychological significance of the personality; 3. General interests of the personality; 4. Necessities of the personality; 5. Needs of the personality; 6. Moral qualities of the personality; 7. Individual aspirations. These aspects unify the values of a personality.

All individuals differ from each other; however, they are brought together in the character of the whole nation. Therefore, we conclude in saying that "... individual personality characteristics form a group of character traits in expressing general views of social life within the Soviet society."(8) " Many human values of the Soviet collective depend on direct human contacts and the human interrelationship of friendship, intellectual unity, a conscious responsibility, the willpower of the whole collective and its moral aspirations."(9) In addition, the formation of communist ideals of the personality depend on the degree of emotions and feelings which enrich the inner world of the personality. Moral ideals and emotions of the personality are interrelated. The communist ideal of life has to be absorbed as a personal conviction by all individuals; it has to be unified not only with knowledge, but also with man's emotions and feelings, and it has to stimulate an inner need of man to fight for these ideals. However, this requires a purposeful development of emotions of all individuals who are in conformity with communist principles. In developing moral feelings and emotions of people, we find serious deficiencies which are expressed through a weak theoretical concept in formulating moral views and emotions. The major conflict exists however, between emotionality and rationality of the personality structure. The perfection of man is not as much directed toward the enrichment of his consciousness or the perfection of his mind, but toward the enrichment of his emotions. " Some people have strong emotions of collectivism which they express through the production process within a collective. The emotional expression of communist ideals influences the feelings of personality while at the same time, it unifies man's willpower and mind in a belief system. Man's emotional capacity assists the personality structure in building the communist morality."(10)

Specific moral values are defined as a form of social consciousness. Morality incorporates the emotions and the mind of man, as well as man's willpower in developing organic knowledge, and the understanding of behavioral principles and emotions, which are related to the realization of such principles. The moral aspect of human existence appears as an assimilated personality, as its inner regulatory mechanism. Morality regulates the behavior of man through individual consciousness. The personality has, in relationship to moral principles, a free selectivity. The mastering of social norms and the evaluation of such norms depends on personal perception. " The evaluation process of the personality determines the moral norms which are viewed in the context between the moral norm and the behavior of an individual."(11)

R E F E R E N C E S

1. Materialy 22. s'ezda KPSS, Moskva, Politizdat, 1961, p. 411.
2. A.G. Kharchev, O dialektiki protsessa vospitaniya. Filosofskie nauki, 1971, No. 1. p. 4.

3. B.D. Parygin, _Sotsial'naya psikhologiya kak nauka_.Lenizdat, 1965, p. 118.
4. O.P. Tselikova, _Kommunisticheskiy ideal i nravstvennoe razvitiye lichnosti_. Moskva, Nauka, 1970, p. 96.
5. O.P. Tselikova, p. 100.
6. _Rabochiy klass i tekhnicheskiy progress_. Moskva, 1966, p. 134.
7. Ibid. p. 147.
8. Ibid. p. 161.
9. A.F. Shishkin, _Osnovy marksistkoy etiki_. Moskva, p. 454.
10. Ibid. p. 177.
11. T.G. Akmambetov, _Problemy nravstvennogo razvitiya lichnosti_. Alma-Ata, Izdatel'stvo " Nauka ", Kazakhskoy SSR, 1971, p. 160.

4. THE MARXIST CONCEPT OF FREEDOM AND PERSONALITY VALUES

From the standpoint of Marxist philosophy, the concept of freedom is actualized in the relationship between man and the universe. It reflects the activities of man and the objective laws of nature and society. " Freedom means man's dominance over nature; it is accomplished by cognitive thinking and material activity. Man is not born free, he has to conquer freedom during the process of practical activities and through the establishment of his personal power in the world. Therefore, freedom is not an absolute category. Freedom is inseparable from necessity. We can comprehend the dialectical essence of freedom only in connection with objective necessities, and in connection with its origin and development."(1)

A most recent Soviet theoretical view on freedom was presented by M.V. Demin in saying that " the subjective realization of freedom is accomplished through the possibility of making consciously an independent choice. The freedom of choice, as well as all other aspects of freedom, is based on knowledge. Inner freedom presents only one aspect of freedom, which is not realized or incorporated in the experience of life, or in activity. Inner freedom appears in the consciousness of man. However, true freedom in its final form is the practical mastery of necessity."(2)

V.E. Davidovich gave the following interpretation on the essence of personal freedom. "... The theoretical essence of personal freedom lies in the presentation of the concrete historical nature of the personality, in the character of its goals in life, in analyzing the objective possibilities of choice and in the achievement of desired goals of individual existence."(3)

The Soviet interpretation of ' freedom of the personality ' is based on the analysis of the subject of personality. Freedom of personality has many different interpretative variations which are visible at various levels of the social strata, for example, economic freedom of the personality, spiritual freedom of the personality, and political freedom of the personality. All these aspects of freedom form a united structure of freedom of man. The accomplishments of exploring space are the result of the freedom of man. Freedom of man is also the result of free activity of many collective personalities and their freedoms. ' Freedom of the personality ', can be further defined as ' democratic freedom of the personality ', freedom of the personality of citizens. V.I. Lenin defined ' freedom of citizen ' as an aspect of the freedom of the personality, " As freedom of family life, as freedom of personal aspirations, as freedom of the personality."(4)

The activities of man can be called free, if he acts under the guidance of functional laws of his organism, and if he is able to control his dreams, his leisure time and his work. The practical realization of freedom of the personality depends on the level of realization of objective conditions within a society. If the social-political and economic conditions in the society are without suppression and exploitation, one will encounter objective conditions for the liberalization of the personality. The subjective aspects of the personality are activity, consciousness, the responsibility of the personality, and a strong willpower in all human activities. " Subjective and objective conditions of freedom exist in a dialectical relationship, in a unity of mutual interdependence."(5) " Spiritual freedom, however, can be achieved with social consciousness, which functions as a regulator of practical activities of the subject. Spiritual freedom contributes to the behavior characteristics and to the realization of life expectations. Freedom further appears as an attributative quality of mankind, as a historical necessity, and by realizing social reality in all aspects of application: in labor relations, in economic relations, political relations, legal relations and in spiritual life. Freedom is a developing process."(6)

The expansion of freedom of the personality depends on the growth of the personality. The accountability of the personality is possible under conditions of freedom and self-determination. If man is not free, he will be unable to take the necessary responsibility for his actions. If a person makes a decision based on his personal free will and in conformity with his work and in conformity with the best interests of the society, then he will have to take the necessary responsibility for his actions. Responsibility on the other hand presupposes a detailed appraisal of choice and of self-imposed decisions. " To be responsible or to take any kind of responsibility, means, to foresee the consequences of one's actions and behavior which is always ready to respond to one's impulses."(7)

The world view of man relates to reality and characterizes the degree and type of development of man's capabilities, his social orientation and his inner freedom. " Human nature characterizes the economic and cultural activities and forms the freedom of the personality, which is linked with the formation process of the scientific-world outlook."(8) The communist world outlook applies the results of freedom of the personality within the practical struggle for such freedom, between the historical process of ideas and the creation of social conditions of life. Man finds the purpose of life, his freedom and his humanistic aspirations in the daily struggle. The scientific methodology of Marxism-Leninism, its revolutionary spirit and the characteristics of the communist world outlook, like criticism, are of significance for the development of the inner freedom of the personality. The inner discrepancies of the personality, the freedom in activity and its social activities are unable to exist without a critical relationship toward reality, toward personal behavior. Such a critical approach was originally incorporated into the communist world outlook and is associated with its revolutionary character. However, there is a difference between anarchical concept of freedom of personality and its critique and the political party, which is aimed at reorganizing the society. The socialist society on the other hand, creates and develops objective tendencies, which serve progress in the realm of freedom. This process is realized in removing internal contradictions of the freedom of the personality.

Freedom of the will is the result of materialist concepts of social determinism. However, moral and ethical freedom of the personality depend on the degree of freedom existing in the society and from other aspects of freedom, for example, freedom of consciousness, freedom of creativity and spiritual freedom. The inner freedom of man is linked with the perception of freedom of the will. Borovskiy defines freedom of the personality in saying that " determinism is characterized mainly by the perception and the emotions of inter-personal and moral-psychological freedom of the personality which enables the subject through the process of motivation to obtain its choice and to achieve its accepted purpose."(9) " The precondition of free choice is the knowledge of cognitive activities of man which are based on his material-emotional and practical activities... The freedom of the will is formed with the capability of solving problems through work."(10) Spiritual freedom appears through social consciousness, as a regulator of practical activities of the subject; spiritual freedom plays an important role in choosing the behavior of man and in choosing the means of realizing its goals."(11)

The world view of man relates to reality; it characterizes the level of man's capabilities, his goal in life, and his social involvement which are related to the inner freedom of man. The following factors form the core of the inner freedom of man, " The knowledge of exterior necessities, individual beliefs and personal interests, the concept of the will and the degree of self-realization."(12)

R E F E R E N C E S

1. K. Marx, F. Engels, Sochineniya, Tom 20, p. 116.
2. M.V. Demin, <u>Problemy teorii lichnosti</u>. Izdatel'stvo Moskovskogo universiteta, 1977, p. 189.
3. V.E. Davidovich, <u>Problemy chelovecheskoy svobody</u>. L'vov, 1967, p. 66.
4. V.I. Lenin, Poln. sobr. soch., tom 7, p. 134.
5. T. Sarsenbayev, <u>Sotsializm i svoboda lichnosti</u>. Izdatel'stvo Kazakhstana, 1969, p. 10.

6. O.G. Drobnitskiy, Mir ozhivshikh predmetov. Problemy tsennostey i marksistkaya filosofiya. Moskva, Politizdat, 1967.
7. L.V. Nikolayeva, Ob'yektivnye i sub'yektivnye faktory sotsial'nogo progressa i svobodi. Izdatel'stvo Moskovskogo universiteta, 1974, p. 270.
8. V.I. Stemkovskaya, Sotsializm i svoboda. Akademiya Nauk, Institut Filosofii, Izdatel'stvo " Nauka ", Moskva, 1975, pp.96-97.
9. M.I. Borovskiy, Determinizm i nravstennoe povedenie lichnosti. Akademiya Nauk Belorusskoy SSR, Institut Filosofii i prava. Izdatel'stvo Nauka i Tekhnika, Minsk, 1974, p. 223.
10. A.G. Myslivchenko, O vnutrenney svobode cheloveka. In: Problema cheloveka v sovremennoy filosofii. Akademiya Nauk, Institut Filosofii, Izdatel'stvo " Nauka ", Moskva, 1969, p. 256.
11. L.V. Nikolayeva, p. 129.
12. V.I. Stempkovskaya, p. 96.

5. PERSONALITY OF SOVIET MILITARY LEADERS

The psychological formation process of personality models of Soviet military leaders is brought about by combining psychological features (character traits, temperament, sharpness of mind and personal interests) in each individual as a constant unity which can be viewed as a permanency of the mental makeup of a personality. This constancy is related to a permanency of the aggregate of social relations in which the person is involved and which constitute the personality, as well as the conditions of life, and particular features of physical appearance. However, the designated permanency is relative. Changes in the mental makeup of the personality have been disclosed in many Soviet psychological investigations. These changes occur under conditions of a person's existence and his private or military activity, and are determined primarily by the process of social interchange.

A special role is played by the authority of a commander in the army. In terms of its purpose and specific features of organization, the army is inconceivable without subordinating the will of the masses to the will of one person. V.I. Lenin considered unity of command in the army to be the most effective method of troop command and control. In his opinion, " more than anything else provides the best use of human capabilities and a real and not verbal check on the work."(1)

Under the present political and military policy, the Soviet commanders responsibilities have even increased. Modern combat requires an unprecedented stress on all physical and moral capabilities of troops, as well as the greatest efficiency in making decisions and their quick execution.Under these conditions, the firm will of a commander,his mastery, organizational capabilities, and ability to influence the minds and hearts of his subordinates are of great significance.

The CPSU views unity of command as the most important principle in the organizational development of the Soviet Armed Forces. The particular feature of unity of command is that it is developed and strengthened on a Party basis, and assumes full force and provides the best results when the sole commander relies upon support of the Party and Komsomol organizations and entire military collective.

Authority is necessary for Soviet soldiers and officers to successfully undertake military and political actions. It enables the commander of military units to more efficiently use the options of military leadership, which increases military preparedness.

A.A. Grechko, former Defense Minister of the USSR, pointed out that " the efforts of a commander, his style of activities, depend largely on his military and political training, since his military discipline is a reflection of the values of his personality characteristics. The commander in the Soviet Armed Forces is granted unlimited power, which is necessary for the execution of his complex duties and responsibilities."(2)

The authority of a Soviet commander depends on socioeconomic and political conditions. The Communist Party gives him many privileges and specific powers, as well as important responsibilities and duties. The authority of a commander within the concept of sociopsychological conditions and in connection with social and objective aspects, has also a psychological aspect, which can reinforce his authority. In this connection, M.I. Kalinin wrote, that " it is essential that the Komsomol officer be respected not only as a lieutenant or captain, but as an expert in his job, a rational man, and a political leader. In other words, he should win authority, and win it primarily by knowledge and experience."(3) The development of leadership authority involves a long and painstaking process, which requires many efforts and concentration, a general self-improvement, a constant analysis of one's activities, personal conduct and relations with others. However, a complete and correct notion of the typical personality of a military leader cannot be obtained without considering the degree of his authoritativness, which in many ways is determined by his basic human qualities, that is, moral-political, professional, and organizational. The following basic personality qualities are inherent to true military authority:

1. Ideological conviction, moral consciousness -activity within sociopolitical life of the subunit or unit.
2. Professional preparedness, extensive knowledge of military affairs, and good military-technical preparation.
3. A love for one's profession, as well as a responsible and creative attitude toward the job.
4. Moral purity, that is: honesty, justness, industriousness, humility, and proper conduct in everyday life and in the family.
5. Organizational capabilities, professionalism, practical awareness, and the ability to promptly spot and support all that is new and advanced.
6. Discipline, efficiency, purposefulness, initiative, restraint, self-possession, tenacity, daring, and the ability to endure the hardships and deprivations of military service.
7. Tactfulness, great exactingness combined with concern, justness and respect for personal dignity of man- absence of nervousness, irritability, impetuosness, and arrogance.
8. Pedagogical thought and pedagogical skill.
9. The ability to rely on the Party and Komsomol organizations and on the community ."(4)

In pointing out personal qualities and personality characteristics which determine and form the true authority of an Soviet military officer, we have to mention his ability to promptly make a sound decision during a critical moment of a complex combat or service situation and to carry it out without allowing hesitation and argument. A great role is played by his firmness, purposefulness and tenacity, strong will, ability to demand from subordinates unfailing execution of their duties, as well as orders and instructions, and thoughtfulness, a desire to understand the psychology of the collective, each soldier and sergeant, a desire to soberly judge successes and failures, and the ability to draw a lesson for the future from each mistake. It is important that the officer not be afraid to learn from his subordinates or assimilate their experience and knowledge. All of this provides for his success in activities, as well as for true respect and authority among the men.

a. The Directiveness of the Soviet Military Personality

The directiveness of the personality of the Soviet military personnel is a process within the general structure of the personality, since it includes different interrelated components. The directiveness of the Soviet military personality includes: the level of its spiritual and intellectual maturity, intensity, moral stability, and effectiveness. The level of maturity of the directiveness of a specific personality represents the social significance of the basic desire of a soldier, his ideological position, his moral and political makeup, and the level of his ideological loyalty. The intensity of the directiveness of a soldier's personality incorporates obscure drives, desires, aspirations, and personal conviction.

Actions of war and aggressiveness influence a person and subject him to the strongest testing of his ideological principles, as well as his personality qualities and the firmness of his convictions. An enemy can be resisted only by an ideologically strong soldier, with a strong moral-political and military-professional directiveness of his personality, and without contradictions of his aspirations. The most stable directiveness of a personality may not be manifested in the deeds and actions of a soldier if its effectiveness is weak. The effectiveness of a personality's directiveness is the actualization of the ideological motivation of a soldier. This fact is manifested in the degree of volitional activity of the personality in carrying out its goals and intentions. The effectiveness depends on the stability of motives which lead the soldier in his activities of killing. Therefore, the most essential and basic process in the indoctrination of a Soviet soldier is the creation of a firm and effective military-professional directiveness. This fact holds the lead in the overall structure of a military personality, and determines the purpose and moral makeup of a soldier and his value to society.

REFERENCES

1. V.I. Lenin, Polnoe sobranie sochinenii, Vol. 40, p. 76. Izd.5. Moskva, Gos.izd-vo polit.Lit-ry, 1958-1965.
2. A.A. Grechko, _Na strazhe mira i stroitel'stva kommunizma_. p. 85, Moskva, Voenizdat, 1971.
3. M.I. Kalinin, _O komm. vospitanii i voinskom dolge_. Sostavil M.V. Kabanov, Moskva, Voen.izd-vo, 1967, p. 625.
4. _Military Psychology, A Soviet View_. Edited by V.V. Shelyag, A.D. Glotochkin, K.K. Platonov, Translated and published under the auspices of the United States Air Force, 1976, p. 312.

C. APPLIED SOVIET PERSONALITY VALUES

1. LEISURE AND NON-WORKING TIME IN THE USSR AND PERSONALITY DEVELOPMENT

Marx considered free time " a basic criterion of the wealth of communist society, because it is a prerequisite for the comprehensive development of the personality."(1)

In the context of the scientific-technological revolution, the function of leisure time acquires ever increasing importance. By ensuring the continuing satisfaction of the physical and cultural needs of each individual, it promotes an increase in productivity at work, easier and more rapid assimilation into new professions, and full participation in the life of the Soviet society.

During the past 20 years, working time has been continuosly shortened, and by 1965 the 40 hour weekly working time structure was instroduced. A.N. Kosygin pointed out at the 23rd Party Congress of the CPSU, that with the introduction of the new Five Year Plan the five day work week has been initiated, which gives the workers sufficient time for rest, study and relaxation.

The current Soviet official interest in leisure time and non-working time is a by-product of the concern with the younger generation. Free time plays much a greater part in the lives of the young than in those of adults, and the ways they spend this time have a lasting influence upon the formation of their character. In examining the expenditure of free time by Soviet citizens, we can find interesting information in the time-budget studies designed to obtain a detailed picture of how selected groups of citizens spent their free and non-working time.

Rapid changes within the Soviet society have accelerated the process of leisure time activities. Such social changes are of significance for the development and improvement of the personality structure. The answers of the questionnaire study of Table III. indicate the leisure time structure of the urban population. The activities belonging to leisure time may be divided into several groups: The first includes study and self-education, various forms of individual and group assimilation

Table III.

NON-WORKING TIME SCHEDULE OF SOVIET PEOPLE*

Type of activities	1	2	3	4
1. Civic work	16.6	21.5	34.2	5.5
2. Political education	3.0	19.0	19.6	1.2
3. Evening and correspondence courses	20.2	-	-	-
4. Self-education	9.1	10.1	17.6	5.0
5. Reading newspapers	81.6	7.7	1.2	0.4
6. Reading journals	36.2	22.3	13.8	1.1
7. Reading books	54.8	14.8	5.7	2.1
8. Listening to radio	70.9	8.0	3.7	0.4
9. Watching TV	15.9	21.6	7.8	1.8
10. Going to movies	0.2	44.6	28.5	8.6
11. Going to theatre	-	2.2	19.2	20.8
12. Going to concerts and literary recitals	-	1.1	6.5	10.2
13. Going to variety shows	-	1.8	11.6	23.2
14. Visiting museums	0.3	0.7	5.2	17.2
15. Visiting sports events	-	10.7	11.9	9.4
16. Hobbies	3.6	8.2	9.2	4.6
17. Hikes, outings	1.2	5.8	12.2	11.9
18. Promenades	25.3	19.4	9.4	4.0
19. Devoting time to children	34.7	5.8	2.1	1.2
20. Visiting relates and friends, entertaining guests	6.3	29.1	28.7	11.0
21. Dancing	0.8	11.0	9.6	4.8
22. Playing cards	2.1	3.7	3.3	1.9
23. Chess, dominoes	9.5	18.2	9.8	3.3
24. Frequenting restaurants, bars, cafes	0.5	3.1	10.1	8.9
25. Passive rest	22.4	5.7	1.9	1.0
26. Practicing religion	1.6	0.4	0.4	1.1
27. Idling	2.3	1.8	1.3	0.2

1. Every day
2. Several times a week
3. Several times a month
4. Less than once a month

* B. Grushin, Problems of Free Time in the USSR. Progress publishers, Moscow, 1967, p. 43.

of culture, such as attending public performances, visiting museums, reading books and periodicals, listening to radio and watching TV. Another group of leisure activities consists of amateur and public activities, physical culture and sports, tourism and excursions. Another group involves social gatherings with friends and playing with children. An additional portion of leisure time is spent for passive rest and personal desires, romances and emotional involvement. Political education showed the lowest percentage of support or interest with only 3% of daily leisure or non-working time activities. However, the reading of newspapers (81.1%), reading of journals (36.2%), reading of books (54.8%), listening to radio programs (70.9%), watching TV (15.9%), received the highest percentage rate of all answers with regard to the distribution of free and leisure time activities. Such activities can also be interpreted as political education through the means of mass-media. The answers further suggest that Soviet citizens are quite dependent on major sources of public information, which they seem to be absorbing without sufficient criticism. Large percentages of the daily routine allotted for leisure time activities is used for personal or private activities or even for productive activities.

Religious worship is given with 1.6% of daily free time, which is half the time spent on political education. Daily cultural activities received the lowest percentage of answers with regard to visiting museums, movies, theatres and other cultural events. However, the percentage of cultural activities increases rapidly in the fourth group, where cultural activities are pursued several times a month. In addition, Table III. strongly emphasizes the characteristics of the Soviet-Slavic personality, specifically the aspect of sociability of the Soviet people, which is expressed through frequenting restaurants, bars, coffee houses, public dances, playing cards, promenades, hiking, visiting friends and having guests, and outings.

An analysis of Table III. identifies three major categories of personality orientation with regard to given answers. 1.The social aspect of the personality (socialization through emotional expressions). 2. Cultural desires. 3. Political education through mass-media and other means of mass and public information.

a. Weekly Use of Non-Working Time of People with Different Family Status

The weekly use of non-working time of people with different family status is illustrated in Table IV. The total weekly hours spent for preparation of food, shopping, child care, apartment search, personal activities, etc., averages 6 hours less for people or families who enjoy the assistance of family members, as compared to those without the assistance and help of family members for the indicated social necessities.

Apartment search and child care received proportionally the highest percentage of non-working time; the weekly hours spent for personal needs are almost equal in comparison of families with and without the assistance of family members. The time spent shopping for groceries is extremely high if compared with Western standards. However, most of the shopping time spent in the USSR is due to waiting in long lines for particular food items, as well as for travel to proper grocery stores, bakery, butchery, etc., before actual shopping can begin. The weekly time spent for apartment search is high if compared with West European and American housing situation. The result of such a tremendous waste of time can be linked to the severe housing problem in the USSR. The average figure of 3.3 weekly hours for apartment search would equal annually 178.2 hours. The time spent in search for shoes and clothing, as well as for other consumer items, is 50% less than the time needed for apartment search. The analysis of Table IV. illustrates a rather critical, socially motivated personality structure of the contemporary Soviet society. The socially critical aspect of the personality is influenced by consumer demands and consumer availability. The answers in Table IV. further indicate basic human needs of average Soviet families, which are typified by socially motivated personality characteristics. It should also be noted, that most of the social necessities mentioned in Table IV. are secured by women, who perform these duties in addition to their regular weekly working time.

b. Changes in Using Non-Working time for Material and Social Necessities of Workers from 1960-1980

The comparative analysis of the weekly time schedule of non-

Table IV.

WEEKLY USE OF NON-WORKING TIME OF PEOPLE WITH DIFFERENT FAMILY STATUS OF THE KRASNOYARSK KRAI (IN HOURS)*

Time schedule	No children	One child	Two children	Three or more
A. With the assistance of family members				
1. Shopping	3.1	3.5	2.9	3.3
2. Preparation of food	2.6	2.6	1.8	3.1
3. Search for apartment and furniture	3.5	3.1	3.3	3.4
4. Search for clothing, shoes and linen	1.5	1.6	1.0	1.1
5. Child care	-	4.3	3.9	5.0
6. Taking care of one self	4.0	4.2	4.0	4.2
7. Various other duties	7.2	7.5	9.6	10.1
Total hours	21.9	26.8	26.4	30.2
B. Without the assistance of family members				
1. Shopping	4.6	4.8	4.4	5.4
2. Preparation of food	6.3	7.1	7.0	8.4
3. Search for apartment and furniture	3.7	3.2	3.5	4.3
4. Search for clothing, shoes and linen	2.2	2.3	3.0	3.0
5. Child care	-	5.4	7.9	7.5
6. Taking care of one self	4.5	4.1	4.4	3.9
7. Various other duties	6.2	4.0	5.0	5.6
Total hours	27.5	30.9	35.2	38.1

* V.I. Bolgov, Vnerabochee vremya i uroven' zhizni trudyashchikhsya. Akademiya Nauk SSSR, Sibirskoe otdelenie, Institut ekonomiki i organizatsii promyshlennogo proizvodstva, Novosibirsk, 1964, p. 59.

working time for material and social necessities of workers of the Krasnkyarsk Krai in 1960-1980 appears as follows: The total hours of non-working time spent by men in 1960 for shopping, preparation of food, search for apartment, child care and personal necessities was 21.0 hours as compared to 13.5 hours in 1980, with a total improvement of the weekly non-working time budget of 7 hours, during a period of 20 years. This positive change in the weekly non-working time schedule gives Soviet workers more time to attend their private and personal needs; it further confirms a slow tendency in improving social relations and social services within contemporary Soviet society. (Table V.)

The comparison for women is even more optimistic. In 1960, women spent a total of 39.6 hours weekly for social necessities, as compared to 15.0 hours in 1980. The improvement of the non-working time schedule is seen in less time spent by women for child care, searching for clothes, searching for apartments, preparing food and shopping. This positive trend for the use of non-working time is the result of scientific-technological innovations, better housing facilities, and a better supply of food. The changes in the non-working time schedule for workers within the past 20 years have indicated an improvement of time allocation for private and personal needs, for intimate desires and passive relaxation. These factors further stimulate progressive developmental tendencies in the individual personality structure, as well as inter-human relations and general personality values.

c. The Use of Weekly Leisure Time of Workers in Relationship to Their Educational Background

The educational background significantly influences the individual attitudes of workers with regard to their leisure time activities. The time spent for studies and self-education by women with a 4th grade education is ten times lower than time spent by educated women or women with unfinished higher education. General and passive relaxation however, is 50% higher for uneducated women that the leisure time of educated women, which is seen in the fact that professional women have to pursue their careers and professional improve-

Table V.

CHANGES IN USING NON-WORKING TIME FOR MATERIAL AND SOCIAL NECESSITIES OF WORKERS FROM 1960-1980 (WEEKLY TIME ALLOCATION AS COMPUTED FOR ONE PERSON)*

	1960				1980			
	Men		Women		Men		Women	
Time Budget	Hours	% of total	Hours	% of total	Hours	% of total	Hours	% of total
1. Shopping	3.2	15.3	5.2	13.1	3.0	22.2	3.5	23.3
2. Preparation of food	2.0	9.5	11.0	27.8	1.0	7.4	1.2	8.0
3. Search for apartment and furniture	2.8	13.3	5.0	12.6	2.0	14.9	2.0	13.3
4. Search for clothing, shoes and linen	1.0	4.8	4.8	12.0	1.0	7.4	1.0	6.7
5. Child care	3.3	15.7	4.7	11.9	1.0	7.4	1.3	8.7
6. Taking care of one self	4.2	20.0	4.4	11.1	4.5	33.3	5.0	33.3
7. Other duties	4.5	21.4	4.5	11.4	1.0	7.4	1.0	6.7
Total	21.0	100.0	39.6	100.0	13.5	100.0	15.0	100.0

* V.I. Bolgov, *Vnerabochee vremya i uroven' zhizni trudyashchisya*. Akademiya Nauk SSSR, Sibirskoe otdelenie, Institut ekonomiki i organizatsii promyshlennogo proizvodtva, Novosibirsk, 1964, p. 78.

ment during their leisure and non-working time. There is no visible difference with regard to non-working time activities and leisure time activities of educated and uneducated men. The total leisure time budget of uneducated men is weekly 24.5 hours as compared to 33.4 weekly hours of the leisure time schedule of educated men, which makes a difference of about 10 weekly hours of more leisure and non-working time for educated men. The additional 10 hours however, are consumed by self-education, studies and professional improvement of educated men. (Table VI.)

The development of individual personality values and individual personality characteristics is influenced by the level of education and professional performance of Soviet workers and professionals. Higher and advanced education help form a keener awareness of individual consciousness and individual attitudes towards personal beliefs and private desires. Such a developmental tendency promotes independent volitional qualities which influence the personality structure of creative thinking people, who are not hesitant in making their own decisions of how to spend their non-working and leisure time and how to improve both their social status and their inner-spiritual values.

d. The Weekly Time Schedule of Engineers of the Krasnoyarsk Krai

The weekly time schedule of engineers and technical personnel in 1963, as compared to the time schedule for 1959 (Table VII.), illustrates important changes which occured after the shortening of the working day and the total weekly working hours. The actual improvement, with regard to free and leisure time, was for men 5.6 weekly hours, and for women 4.3 weekly hours during the time span from 1959 to 1963. The leisure time structure of engineers and technicians for 1959 varied between 15.3 to 25 weekly hours (without a day off) for men; for women, however, from 10.6 to 16 weekly hours, which gives us a weekly average of 20.7 hours for men and 11.7 hours for women. The percentage of weekly time structure, without a day off, shows 14.3% for men and 8.1% for women of non-working time. Under the

Table VI.

THE USE OF WEEKLY LEISURE TIME OF WORKERS IN RELATIONSHIP TO THEIR EDUCATIONAL BACKGROUND (ANALYSIS OF THE KRASNOYARSK KRAI)*

LEISURE TIME SCHEDULE	Up to fourth grade				5-9 grade				Highschool and unfinished higher education			
	Men		Women		Men		Women		Men		Women	
	Hours	%	Hours	%	Hours	%	Hours	%	Hours	%	Hours	%
1. Studies	1.3	5.3	0.6	4.3	4.4	15.2	3.6	17.0	7.6	22.8	8.2	31.0
2. Self-education	5.4	22.0	1.9	13.5	7.2	24.8	4.0	19.0	8.3	24.8	5.3	20.0
3. Gymnastics and sport	1.2	4.9	-	-	1.4	4.8	0.1	0.5	1.2	3.6	0.5	2.0
4. Entertainment	12.7	51.9	3.4	59.6	12.2	42.1	10.0	47.4	12.5	37.4	10.0	38.0
5. Hobbies	0.2	0.8	0.2	1.4	0.3	1.0	0.2	0.9	0.3	0.9	0.3	1.1
6. Social participation	0.3	1.2	0.5	3.5	0.2	0.7	0.4	1.9	0.5	1.5	0.8	3.0
7. Relaxation	2.1	8.6	1.2	8.5	2.0	6.9	1.8	8.5	1.8	5.4	0.6	2.3
8. Other activties	1.3	5.3	1.3	9.2	1.3	4.5	1.0	4.7	1.2	3.6	0.7	2.0
Total of the leisure time structure	24,5	100.0	14.1	100.0	29.0	100.0	21.1	100.0	33.4	100.0	26.4	100.0

* Bolgov, V.I. Vnerabochee vremya i uroven' zhizni trudyashchisya. Akademiya Nauk SSSR, Sibirskoe otdelenie, Institut ekonomiki i organizatsii promyshlennogo proizvodstva. Novosibirsk, 1964, p. 116.

influence of the shorter working day in 1963, the leisure time structure varied from 20.4 hours to 27.7 weekly hours for men and 10.3 to 19.2 weekly hours for women. An average time schedule of 24.8 weekly hours for men in leisure time activities, 17.2% of the total weekly time structure, and 14.4 weekly hours for women, or only 10.0% of the total weekly time structure.

The non-working time related to production and work at home represent combined 20.9 weekly hours, which are lost to the leisure time structure of engineers. The actual weekly working time schedule was 67.3 hours weekly for engineers for 1963, which is almost half the total weekly time structure. Computed on a daily basis, the figure of 9.5 hours is devoted to work. The weekly working time schedule for women is even more appalling, with a total of 78.3 weekly working hours, including actual working time, work at home and non-working time related to production. The difference of the actual weekly working time between men and women for 1963 lies in the fact, that women perform housework, cooking, shopping, care for children, etc.

e. Schedule of Leisure Time of Soviet Workers

A comparative analysis of the leisure time schedule of Soviet workers in 1924 and 1959 shows significant improvements in the time allotted for cultural activities. (Table VIII.) In 1924, only 69 hours of cultural activities were available to workers as compared to 408 hours for 1959. Other leisure time activities, such as leisure time activities related to production, amateur activities and sports activities have a lesser degree of change. Leisure time activities for men related to production decreased from 277 annual hours in 1924, to 192 annual hours in 1959. For women, however, we see an increase in total annual hours related to production from 153 in 1924, to 199 in 1959. Amateur activities show another decrease for men, from 464 annual hours in 1924 to 339 annual hours in 1959. For women, another increase in annual hours, from 125 in 1924, to 190 in 1959. Sport activities showed an increase for men, from 119 annual hours in 1924, to 148 annual hours in 1959. For women, the increase in total annual hours for sport activities is minimal, with 68 hours in 1924, to 72 annual hours in 1959. The figure given for time

Table VII.

WEEKLY TIME SCHEDULE OF ENGINEERS OF THE KRASNOYARSK KRAI*

Weekly time schedule	Men		Women	
	1959	1963	1959	1963
1. Working time	52.0	46.4	47.2	42.9
2. Non-working time related to production	9.3	10.0	9.2	9.8
3. Work at home	11.0	10.9	25.5	25.6
4. Aesthetic activities	51.0	51.9	50.4	51.3
5. Leisure time	20.7	24.8	11.7	14.4
Total	144	144	144	144

* V.G. Baykova, A.S. Duchal, A.A. Zemtsov, Ed., *Svobodnoe vremya i vsestoronnee razvitie lichnosti*. Akademiya obshchestvennykh nauk pri TsK KPSS, Kafedra nauchnogo kommunizma. Izdatel'stvo " Mysl' ", Moskva, 1965, p. 154.

wasted during leisure time activities is slightly higher in 1959, as compared to the figures in 1924, with 238 annual hours in 1924 to 254 annual hours in 1959 for men, as compared to 216 annual hours for women in 1924, to 221 annual hours in 1959. Leisure time without activities,or ' passive relaxation ' decreased during the 25 year time period from 381 annual hours in 1924 to 206 annual hours in 1959 for men, and from 277 in 1924 for women as compared to 113 annual hours in 1959. This represents a reduction in the personal time schedule of over 150% for workers from 1924 to 1959. This drastic reduction of time devoted to passive relaxation for Soviet workers is attributable to scientific and technological innovations, to the modernization of the Soviet industry, to the improvement of the Soviet national economy and subsequently to higher consumer demands, which, on the other hand, require more working time. The time lost for passive relaxation has been integrated into the production process of the economy and industry. The amateur activities of workers decreased from 464 annual hours in 1924, to 339 annual hours for men in 1959. However, an increase of annual hours spent for amateur activities for women is astonishing, from 125 annual hours in 1924, to 190 annual hours in 1959. The time schedule for sport activities remained almost unchanged during the 25 year time period.

The Soviet leisure time structure has many inconsistencies: many professionals are not fully engaged in the production process and lag behind engineers, technicians and factory workers; this is the result of the free time, which influences private activities and personal desires, as well as the intimate atmosphere of individual existence.

" Judging from the data obtained, nearly a quarter of the Soviet people do not watch TV, one-tenth does not read newspapers, one sixth does not listen to radio or goes to movies." (2) From the data analyzed in Tables III. through VIII., one is able to conclude that the leisure time structure of workers, professionals, engineers, educated and non-educated Soviet citizens, significantly influences and forms individual personality characteristics and human values. The cross analysis of leisure time and non-working time schedules provides a personality model which is oriented toward industrial and economic change and improvement. The scientific-technological revolution created the contemporary human value system which is, to some

Table VIII.

SCHEDULE OF LEISURE TIME OF SOVIET WORKERS (IN HOURS)*

Leisure time	1924		1959	
	Men	Women	Men	Women
1. Leisure activities related to production	277	153	192	199
2. Amateur activities	464	125	339	190
3. Sport activities	119	68	148	72
4. Cultural relaxation	69	30	408	333
5. Waste of time	238	216	257	221
6. Leisure time (Passive relaxation)	381	277	206	113
Total hours of leisure time	1548	869	1550	1128

* S. Strumilin, <u>Nash mir cherez 20 let</u>. Moskva, 1964, p. 90.

degree, independent from traditional Marxist value concepts. A productive and socially critical individual, as well as a collective personality structure is of prime concern to the Soviet government, for this individual plays a key part in the developing process within contemporary Soviet society. The leisure time structure of Soviet people shows a productive tendency while they maintain their private and personal aspirations, desires, personal beliefs and value concepts, regardless the many restrictions imposed on them by the government.

R E F E R E N C E S

1. K. Marx, F. Engels, Collected Works, 2nd Ed. Vol. 46. Part 2, p. 217.
2. B. Grushin, Problems of Free Time in the USSR. Progress Publishers, Moskva, 1967, p. 44.

Table IX.

DAILY TIME STRUCTURE OF SOVIET WORKERS

- WORKING TIME
  - ACTUAL WORKING TIME
  - NON-PRODUCTIVE USE OF WORKING TIME
  - REGULATED WORK BREAK
- NON-WORKING TIME
  - TIME SPENT IN CONNECTION WITH PRODUCTIVE LABOR
    - LUNCH BREAKS
    - TRAVEL TO AND FROM WORK
    - TIME FOR PRIVATE NEED BEFORE AND AFTER WORK
  - LEISURE TIME
    - PROFESSIONAL IMPROVEMENT AND STUDY
    - WORK FOR THE COMMUNITY
    - SELF-EDUCATION
    - PRIVATE RELAXATION WITH CHILDREN
  - WORK AT HOME
    - TIME SPENT IN ONES OWN HOUSEHOLD
    - TIME SPENT FOR VARIOUS SERVICES
      - SHOPPING PREPARATION OF FOOD
      - CHILD CARE
      - SEARCH FOR HOUSING AND FURNITURE
      - SEARCH FOR CLOTHES, SHOES AND LINEN
      - TIME FOR ONE-SELF
      - OTHER ASPECTS OF HOME WORK
  - SLEEPING AND EATING TIME
    - DAY DREAMS

2. SOVIET ASOCIAL PERSONALITY CHARACTERISTICS

Due to the general lack of household facilities in the Soviet Union and due to the discriminatory attitude towards women in the Soviet society, many educated and professional women are forced to stop working for several years after having children.

The Department of Economics at the Academy of Sciences of the Urals, USSR, conducted a research project in evaluating the social status of women after having children; the research was conducted in five cities and in one rural community of the Chelyabinskiy province. The research results are presented in Table X.

Table X.

WHY ARE PROFESSIONAL WOMEN NOT ABLE TO PURSUE THEIR CAREERS?*

Reason	In cities		Troitskiy Distr.	
	No.	%	No.	%
1. Lack of day-care centers	3206	36.4	900	56.9
2. Looking after school aged children	820	9.4	239	15.5
3. Looking after other members of the family	773	8.7	184	11.9
4. Lack of work	1616	18.2	83	5.4
5. Do not wish to work	1495	17.0	62	4.0
6. Temporary illness	916	10.3	75	4.7
Total	8826	100.0	1543	100.0

* Stroitel'stvo kommunizma i formirovanie novogo cheloveka. Sverdlovskiy gosudarstvennyy pedagogicheskiy institut. Sverdlovsk, 1966. Ministerstvo prosveshcheniya RSFSR, Uchenye zapiski, p. 161.

Table X. indicates that 5166 women interviewed were unable to work and perform positive functions within the society after having children. Half of all work capable women must stay at home (49.8%). The primary reason for the loss of manpower is seen in lack of day-care centers. The availability of day-care centers would create positive results within the general area of social services and family relations, and would 1. improve the general education of children, 2. it would prevent additional losses of the work force and 3. it would prevent a discriminatory attitude towards women.

The absence of day-care centers represents 36.4% or 3206 answers in cities, and 56.9% or 900 answers in the province, as the reason given by women for not working. Additional 17.0% or 1495 women do not want to work (in cities) as compared to 4.0% or 62 women in the rural community. The absence of work represents 18.2% or 1616 women in cities and 5.4% or 83 women in the rural community. The above analyzed social conditions create an asocial atmosphere and destructive emotional and mental structure within the contemporary Soviet society. These factors most definitely influence the structure of personal relations, happiness and individual values, as well as contemporary personality characteristics, which can be described as alienated and frustrated conditions of human existence. The realization of personal desires of women appears to have a negative value orientation within the Soviet social conditions. In summurizing, one can best characterize such a personality structure as asocial, with suppressed personality values.

Additional aspects of an asocial or destructive personality development can be observed in daily family life. Mechanized household equipment contributes significantly to the creation of a leisurely or relaxed family atmosphere. The number of household appliances increased within the past few years in the Soviet Union, eg., vacuum cleaners, washing-machines and refrigerators. But after interviewing 648 household concerning the basic household facilities, one must conclude that the majority of Soviet households do not possess such appliances, due to the high purchase cost.

Table XI. below indicates the number of households (or the number of working women), who have household appliances.

Table XI.

HOUSEHOLD APPLIANCES*

Kind of appliances	No. of households	%
1. Refrigerator, washing-machine, vacuum cleaner	23	3.5
2. Refrigerator, washing-machine	34	5.2
3. Washing-machine, vacuum cleaner	20	3.1
4. Refrigerator, vacuum cleaner	3	0.5
5. Washing-machine	163	25.2
6. Refrigerator	9	1.4
7. Don't have any appliances	396	61.1
Total	648	100.0

* Stroitel'stvo kommunizma i formirovanie novogo cheloveka. Sverdlovskiy gosudarstvennyy pedagogicheskiy institut, Ministerstvo prosveshcheniya RSFSR, Sverdlovsk, 1966, p. 162

Table XI. indicates that 61.1% of all households surveyed do not have any kind of appliances. Only 1.4% of households possess a refrigerator, and 89.4% of households have to buy groceries on a daily basis due to the lack of refrigeration. The washing-machine is owned by 25.2% of interviewed women. The combination of washing-machine, refrigerator, and vacuum cleaners are owned by only 0.5% of interviewed women. The major burden of housework still rests on women's shoulders. The working and professional women, as well as working mothers, must work an additional 3-5 hours daily at home. During weekends the hours of household chores are even longer.

Compared to women, men contribute 1/2 the time to homecare or in connection with needs of the household. However, women who do not work in factories or other enterprises, work an average of 10-12 hours daily at home.

70-80% of the non-working time of Soviet workers, is spent daily on basic chores, such as shopping and personal needs (bathing, going to the hairdresser). Additional time is spent for housework and other functions related to family life. The daily duties performed at home (cooking, cleaning, washing, taking care of children etc.,) are a direct influence on the leisure time structure within the non-working time, and therefore of greater influence on the cultural consciousness of individuals.

In analyzing the time spent by workers at their job in using the canteen,or by using the services of the community centers, the time saved through organized time schedule can be applied for individual entertainment or physical development. (Table XII.)

In 1959, the Institute of Economics and Organization of Industrial Production of the Siberian Section of the Academy of Sciences USSR, conducted a survey to determine the time spent shopping for groceries and other consumer goods. The survey was conducted during normal business hours. The results of the study illustrate the fact that by buying 10 different items, a total of 34.8% of the total shopping time was used, due to waiting in line, fitting, wrapping of the items and paying for the item at the cashier. For buying groceries, the amount of time spent in waiting in line for 10 items was 87.3% of the total time spent in buying groceries.

However, by using factory facilities for some social services, for eating lunch, etc., a significant amout of time is saved, which could be used by individual workers for cultural or personal activities, as well as for leisure time.

In conclusion, the asocial characteristic of wasting time by standing in line in order to buy groceries and other consumer items, generates a typicality for social conditions and a subsequent development and influence upon the mentality of Soviet people; such attitudes form typical behavior patterns of Soviet citizens and their personality traits.

Table XII.

TIME SCHEDULE OF WORKERS IN USING FACTORY FACILITIES FOR VARIOUS SERVICES (% DURING WEEKDAYS WITHIN THE KRASNO-YARSK KRAI*

Aspects of Time Spent	Men	Women
A. Lunch breaks		
1. Eating	90	86
2. Waiting in line for food	10	14
B. Time Spent for Buying Food		
1. Travel to groceries and markets	30	23
2. Time spent at markets and groceries	30	26
3. Waiting in line in department stores and markets	40	51
C. Appointment at Hair-dressers		
1. Appointment at hair-dressers without waiting in line	50	50
2. Waiting in line for hair-dressers	50	50
D. Using Public Bath-Houses		
1. Taking a bath without waiting	60	43
2. Waiting in line for bath-houses	20	29
3. Travel to and from the bath-house	20	28

* V.I. Bolgov, *Vnerabochee vremya i uroven' zhizni trudyashchisya*. Akademiya Nauk SSSR, Novosibirsk, 1964, p. 62.

3. SOVIET LABOR RELATIONS AND PERSONALITY FORMATION

Labor procures all human wealth, and according to Engels this also means that, "... It is the primary basic condition for all human existence and this to such an extent that, in a sense, we have to say: labor creates man himself." (1) The 22nd Party Congress of the CPSU pointed out the direction of future research on labor relations was to take. The Party program has the following to say on the future directions of labor relations:

" Automation and comprehensive mechanization serve as the material basis for the gradual development of socialist labor into communist labor. Technical progress will require higher standards of production and a higher level of the vocational and general education of all working people. The new machinery will be used to radically improve the Soviet people's working conditions, and make them much easier, to reduce the length of the working day, to improve living conditions, eliminate hard physical work and, subsequently, all unskilled labor."(2)

The contemporary development of Soviet labor relations is illustrated in this chapter as it pertains to the personality formation of workers and the type of work performed, the educational background related to professional performance, the conditions of work and the planning of work, as well as positive and negative personality qualities of workers. Current statistical data is used to indicate major shifts within labor relations as it pertains to general social criticism and self-criticism of workers with regard to their work performed.

a. Soviet Workers Evaluate their Working Conditions

Workers and professionals of the Stankoliniya production enterprise have been asked the question" " What do you most like at your work?" The answers are given in Table XIII.

The fourth group of workers in the questionnaire is highly

qualified. These workers are characterized by professionalism, technical interests and the knowledge of the production process, since they deal with new technologies and machinery, as well as with advanced systems approach. The workers of the fourth group developed the desire to perfect their professionalism and to take creative initiative within their professional performance (80%). The workers of the 2nd group are physical laborers; they are concerned about their wages and their material standard (group I. 27%; group II. 26%). The answers further illustrate the need of workers for personal and private desires; predominant is the social factor of labor, such as professional improvement and creative initiative, and independence at work, which are the prime motives for a socially critical personality development. (Group I. 46%; group III.42%; group IV 80%). Organization of labor amd general importance of work received 32% affirmative answers from group IV; workers of the III. group indicate a higher preference for these questions, with 46% and 39% affirmative answers. The importance of worker's collectives is given the highest percentage of answers from group I. of workers, who are unskilled laborers and from group IV. who are highly skilled technical workers. (Group I. 50%; group IV. 49%). The answers of No. 7. and 8. of the questionnaire indicate a refusal of workers to comment on those issues. The reflected criticism can be applied to the stated priorities of working conditions of all answers from No. 1. through No. 6. The variety and the different levels of preference of specific groups of workers, especially with regard to their professional training, indicate a generally self-critical and constructive individual personality qualities in connection with their professional performance or results of work.

The opinions expressed by young workers in characterizing the conditions of work (Table XIV.) in Soviet production enterprises reflect self-conscious personality qualities, individual criticism, independent thinking and a strong desire for personal needs and a critical attitude toward the Soviet society. The analysis of answers pertinent to conditions of work in Table XIV. present a negative picture of social conditions within the society, and a high degree of dissatisfaction with regard to social accomplishments of the working class.

An average of 50% of young workers want to change their place of work or their profession after one year of work

Table XIII.

WHAT DO YOU MOST LIKE AT YOUR WORK?*

Answers in %	I	II	III	IV
1. General importance of work	35	12	39	32
2. Worker's collective	50	18	28	49
3. Creative initiative; the possibility to improve the profession	46	-	42	80
4. Organization of labor	16	-	46	32
5. Independence at work	27	6	30	20
6. Good wages	27	26	30	20
7. Didn't like anything	7	12	5	-
8. Did not answer	2	6	5	9

I. Unskilled laborer
II. Physical laborer
III. Technicians
IV. Highly skilled technical workers

* K.K. Platonov, Ed., Lichnost' i trud. Izdatel'stvo " Mysl' ", Moskva, 1965, p.223.

seniority at a particular production enterprise. Monotonous work received the highest criticism, from 58% of workers with three years of work seniority. The interest in performance at work declined after three years of work to 28%. The critical attitudes of young people, with regard to their profession and with regard to their working conditions within particular production enterprises, is the reflection of poor labor relations and a general disorientation of working class people. A comparatively low percentage of workers thinks that their immediate work has a direct influence on the output capacity of their production enterprise. After one or two years of work seniority, 20% of workers agree with the assumption that their work directly influences the production process of their enterprises. After three years of seniority the affirmative answer with regard to the same question received 35% of answers, or 3% more than during the first 2-3 months period of work at a particular job. After one year of work in a particular enterprise, nearly 50% of workers would be willing to change their place of work. (48% after one year, 45% after two years, and 47% after three years of work seniority). The desire to change one's occupation is strongly emphasized by young workers with three years of work seniority, with a total of 37% of answers. 46% of students at technical and vocational schools consider their immediate work interesting. However, 40% of them stated that their work is monotonous.

The critical evaluation of conditions of work by young Soviet workers reflects individual initiative, their desire to change and improve, as well as a strong dissatisfaction with existing working conditions.

b. Negative Personality Characteristics of Workers

The character traits of young people and workers illustrated in Table XV. are negative personality traits. These negative personality traits and personality descriptions point to a constructive sense of self-criticism by young workers. This self-critical attitude towards behavior models are found here within the framework of human value orientations, and not in connection with political or ideological aspects of prescribed personality models. The personality weaknesses indicated in Table XV. characterize a less controlled behavior model of Soviet citizens than one might expect under the ideological guidelines of the Soviet system and the guidelines of the Communist Party of the USSR.

27% of the answers pointed to the lack of self-control on the part of workers and illustrate a strong approval for willpower characteristics in the Soviet personality. Self-

Table XIV.

YOUNG WORKERS EVALUATE THEIR CONDITIONS OF WORK*

Opinions	Work seniority				
	Students	months	years		
		2-3	1	2	3
1. My work is interesting	46	40	38	23	28
2. My work is monotonous	40	33	50	56	58
3. Given the opportunity, I am prepared to change my place of work	-	32	48	49	47
4. Given the possibility, most people would change their profession	22	24	28	29	37
5. My immediate work influences the final output of the enterprise	-	32	20	20	35

* A.I. Khodakov, Pedagogical Problems of the Formation of the Personality of Young Workers. Sovetskaya Pedagogika, No.9, Sept. 1974, Table 2. Scientific Research Institute for the General Education of Adults of the Academy of Pedagogical Sciences of the USSR.

control is part of discipline which can be achieved through positive social conditions within the society and not by government-imposed and forced methods of response. Smoking and drinking are part of the so called harmful habits, which are part of the contemporary developmental trend of personality characteristics of the Soviet youth. However, such negative habits received only 4% of all answers. It further indicates a strong desire for independent decision-making in both private and professional spheres. Self-control is associated with creative aspects of human activities, as well as with emotional stability. Hot-tempered behavior among young workers can be found in any society, which is the result of emotional vitality. Hot-temperedness was seen by 18% of young workers as a negative personality quality. This relatively high percentage of answers given to hot-temperedness indicates individual, independent and volitional attitudes of people and negates any imposed restrictions within the sphere of personal desires. Impatience, which received 16% of answers, is related to similar behavior as hot-temperedness. The response to lack of concentration was 11% of answers. Therefore, we are able to combine lack of self-control and lack of concentration under the aspect of willpower characteristics of young workers. Arrogance, capricious behavior, rudeness and greed form a separate group of negative personality traits and represent combined a total of 29% of all answers.

Table XV.

NON-DESIRABLE PERSONALITY TRAITS OF YOUNG WORKERS*

1. Lack of self-control	27%
2. Hot-tempered	18%
3. Impatience	16%
4. Lack of concentration	11%
5. Arrogance	10%
6. Capricious behavior	6%
7. Rudeness	5%
8. Greed	4%
9. Bad habits (Smoking, drinking)	4%
10. Laziness	2%

* K.K. Platonov, Ed., O chertakh lichnosti novogo rabochego. Akademiya Nauk SSSR, Institut Filosofii. Izdatel'stvo Akademii Nauk SSSR, Moskva, 1963. Chapter: V.I. Selivanov, Volevye cherty novogo rabochego. p. 34.

c. Positive Personality Qualities of Soviet Workers

The opposite question has been asked: " What is your ideal of man? " - Ideological qualities, moral qualities, intelligence, justice and consciousness were combined in the first category, which received 85% approval by young workers. If, however, ideological qualities would have appeared as a separate question, the percentage of affirmative answers would have been much lower. The third question of Table XVI. received 72% of approval by young people, where sincerity and respectfulness were the positive personality characteristics. Respectfulness and sincerity, on the other hand, are more closely related to justice, intelligence and moral qualities than ideological qualities. If we subtract the percentage of answers of the third question from the first, we receive a total of 13% of all answers for ideological qualities. Good labor relations and discipline received 31% of answers. The level of discipline as a positive value of young workers appears as critical in comparison with the positive personality qualities referred to in the first and third question. Additional 13% of positive values are given as answers of the fourth question. However, no specific explanation has been given as to the personality qualities indicated.

If we compare the negative personality qualities cited by young workers from Table XV. with those in Table XVI., which are characterized as positive personality qualities, we can conclude, that there are far more negative than positive personality qualities present in young workers which influence their behavior. The answers with regard to positive personality qualities of young workers are related to basic concepts of communist ethics and morality; they appear as a pattern-like package of ideological principles and imposed value formations. The negative personality qualities listed in Table XV. indicate a strong tendency of independent criticism and individual decision-making capabilities, since none of these negative qualities is related to communist or Marxist personality concepts.

Table XVI.

WHAT IS YOUR IDEAL OF MAN?*

Answers	%
1. Ideological and moral qualities: intelligence, justice, consciousness	85
2. Good labor relations, discipline	31
3. In relationship to other people: sincerity, respectfulness	72
4. Other positive qualities	13

* K.K. Platonov, Ed., Lichnost' i trud. Izdatel'stvo " Mysl' ", Moskva, 1965, p. 234.

d. Ideological and Political Education of Young Soviet Workers

Ideological and political education does not significantly influence the world outlook of Soviet workers. Only 5% of questioned workers (Table XVII.) were able to participate in mass-political work after they completed courses in political education. 21.8% still prefer to read fiction and 17% expressed the desire to be useful to the society. However, it was not specified what ' useful to the society ' means. 11.1% adopted a critical attitude toward their colleagues and 9.1% became critical toward TV programs. (There is no indication against what specific programs the criticism is directed).

Social criticism and self-improvement characterize socially

active, individual workers, who clearly display independent personality qualities, as illustrated in Table XIII-XVI., with regard to conditions of work, place of work, labor relations and inter-human relations. Only 4.7% of questioned workers read more social-political literature than before the completion of their political and ideological education. The figures strongly suggest that the communist world outlook of Soviet people dissipates rapidly with regard to traditional Marxist human value perception, due to rapid social change and social dynamics of the Soviet society. A critical attitude toward co-workers stresses the importance and possibility of individual initiative, as well as personal aspirations and competitiveness and professional performance. The general characteristics of individual initiative of workers sugesst personality values which are geared toward self-improvement of human existence as a value entity, regardless of the political framework.

Individual initiative, as applied in connection with the analyzed responses of young workers, is an independent phenomenon of capabilities and creativeness. Initiative enhances attitudes of change within society. Initiative is also required to improve working procedures, the organization of labor and innovative management capabilities. It furthers individual analytical thinking and foresees the results of change. " Initiative is part of the human personality; it develops the human character."(1)

Additional positive and negative personality characteristics which have been analyzed in Tables XIII. through XVII., with regard to the process of work and working conditions include: discipline, intelligence, consciousness, sincerity, constructive criticism and professional performance, a critical attitude toward co-workers, organization of labor, independence at work, lack of self-control, lack of concentration, impatience, laziness, hot-temperedness, flexible in adopting contemporary methods of management, and influential in accomplishing the work norms of the production process of enterprises.

R E F E R E N C E S

1. K.K. Platonov, O chertakh lichnosti novogo rabochego. Akademiya Nauk SSSR, Institut Filosofii, Izdatel'stvo Akademii Nauk SSSR, Moskva, 1963, p. 88.

Table XVII.

HOW DID IDEOLOGICAL AND POLITICAL EDUCATION INFLUENCE YOUR POLITICAL AND CULTURAL WORLD VIEW?*

Answers	In %
1. I listen frequently to social-political radio and TV commentaries	22.5%
2. I read fiction	21.8%
3. I want to serve society	17.0%
4. I have the intention to increase my education and political knowledge	11.2%
5. I became critical toward my colleagues	11.1%
6. I became critical toward TV-programs and movies	9.1%
7. I began to participate in social life	8.6%
8. I am able to participate in mass-political work	5.0%
9. I read social-political literature	4.7%

* I.N. Kambalin, Lichnost' i kollektiv. Irkutsk, 1973, p. 133. Irkutskiy gosudarstvennyy universitet imeni A.A. Zhdanova.

4. THE SOVIET SCIENTIFIC-TECHNOLOGICAL REVOLUTION AND PERSONALITY VALUES

The exploration of space opened new dimensions of social interaction within contemporary Soviet society. Space technology initiated qualitative changes of the ' nature-society ' system in relationship to social dynamics. This process is expanding the social scale of human existence, which has already become a cosmic experience of the future. Group dynamics of collectives depend on individual responsibilities and the scientific consciousness of individual scientists. The collective is the ethical microclimate of inter-human relations. The relationship between man and nature, man and his social environment, as well as between man and man enriches the human consciousness of the new space mentality. Within the system of human relations, man himself changes nature. Man does not change because of his influence upon nature, but because of the powerful influence of the changing nature upon man. " The influence of scientific-technological accomplishments upon the biological and psychological nature of man indicates a change of human existence. The process of change was initiated by the development of computers and the competition of the two world systems, where different percentions of human existence are realized and where different influences characterize the social structure of the contemporary personality."(1)

The mechanisms of interaction between social, biological and human factors are:

1." Biological factors: human activties in ruling over nature; in developments of nature and in activities of human beings.
2. Social factors: technological and productive activities within the social environment.
3. Human factors: the influence of scientific-technological innovations and the technological influence upon the biological, psychological and social characteristics of man and his behavior modifications."(2)

The interrelationship among these three concepts belongs to the developing process of man and society. The man-machine relationship is based on concrete social conditions of the organization of labor and the social nature of man. " The engineering-psychology is guided by the assumption that the accomplishments of technological work of computers will always be subordinated to the conscious work of man, since man is considered the subject of labor."(3)

The application of cybernetic systems and the personal involvement of technicians represents a new social-psychological aspect of existence. However, of importance are problems of " optimal coordination of opportunities for operators of advanced technological systems."(4) Forecasting and future planning of the production collective is part of the management system. Group dynamics, the Soviet term for the psychology of collective behavior, directly relates in obtaining information and management expertise. This relationship provides insight into the cooperation between technicians and the social-psychological micro-climate, which sets the rules for the internal structure of the collective.

The changing character of contemporary labor is analyzed within cybernetics, as part of the transition of complex automatic systems, which further the reorientation and development of sociological, psychological and ethical categories of man. The analysis of structural and functional expectations of various technological systems makes it necessary to investigate the problem of lifetime goals, from a social point of view. The evaluation of personal expectations has a social-psychological and an ethical character; it helps to clarify the regularity of personality development and the structure of the Soviet technological processes. " The examination of the relationship ' man and machine ', as a typical cybernetic system can only be approached from the point of view of life expectation. Technicians created a new path for human activities. For the computer society, the personality characteristics of human activities are not the result of direct contact with real life objects within the management system, but with the informational model of computer systems. " The dialectics of the interrelationship between man and machine is structured by indirect groups of people and their direct participation in a variety of technological systems."(5) The machine-man relationship is integrated into different spheres of social activities of man. The activities of man as a manipulator of technological systems is determined by general regulations of existence and his social consciousness. The man-machine relationship is also an example of self-managing systems within the concept of self-regulating systems. Man as a link between major systems has to be given the opportunity to develop his optimal capabilities, according to one's individual characteristics. Man is also the goal and the target of all scientific-technological innovations which are related to social phenomena. G.N. Volkov writes, in this connection, " Man is part of the combined labor mechanism. Man is universal and rich with life experiences and therefore able to perform more than just technical function."(6) By applying the cybernetic systems within society, man changes his character, as well as his responsibility, within the society and in relationship to the production process.

The problem of human expectation as an essential link between automatic systems and social progress becomes a moral-psychological problem of personal expectations. " Individual morality is associated with the production process of the socialist society; it gains in significance by determining labor relations and political values."(7)

a. Cybernetic Analysis of Social-Psychological Relations of Man

Within social-psychology, cybernetic methods of social analysis are formulated. " Cybernetic methods are based on the assumption that the results of sociological research and the effective application of mathematical models depend on methodological relations of social cybernetics and on the analysis of the societal structure and its self-regulating system." (8) Basic methodological systems and social-psychological concepts within cybernetics include:

1. Different intellectual communities; psychological characteristics of different social collectives.
2. Behavior motivations of individuals within collectives and the characteristics of activities of members of different social groups.
3. Communication methods and social-psychological intercourse

between individual and the group.

4. The rules of collective behavior." (9)

Different structures of the intellectual community and the psychological characteristics of different social collectives are analyzed by the systemic-structural method. " The structural unit of the collective is an ' association of people ', containing the symptons of social groups and social organizations."(10) A collective is the fusion of social groups and organizations; it contains objective (essential) and subjective (organizational) characteristics. In addition, informational values and personal relations have to be applied. N. Viner describes the informational value of life in saying that, "... to live a real life, means, to properly apply informational values."(11) The mechanism of social-psychological communication and behavior is formed with cybernetic aspects of the contemporary information theory. It would be impossible for the Soviet scientists to explore and analyze the importance of social-psychological phenomena without the application of theoretical-informational and cybernetical analysis, which examines public opinion, social development and criticism, the general interests of citizens and necessities of the community.

The personal orientation of people is formed under the influence of informational values, which are transmitted through other people. Science and technology are changing the structure of the contemporary world, as well as the conception of people; this is formed by one's unique spiritual potential, which forms the inner-spiritual and intellectual values of man. Consequently, we consider scientific-technological progress as the essence of the personality formation and as a creative power. The development of the personality structure is a basic problem of the scientific-technological revolution; personality development appears as a contemporary problem not as an ideal phenomena or philosophical interpretation of value formations. The linkage between man and machine is also characterized by moral personality qualities and by moral and psychological reliability of the personality. The effectiveness of automation is determined not by the level of knowledge of man, but by the degree of personal responsibility, the degree of consciousness and personal initiative and the mental condition of workers who operate the control panel

(automated management system).

" The social impact of the scientific-technological revolution determines the position of the moral reliability of the personality. The scientific-technological revolution enables man to utilize the powers of nature by increasing duty and responsibility among people, who apply modern technology and manage the production and technological development." (12) Reliability of the personality is intertwined with the principle of humanization of work and the depiction of communist ideas. Moral-psychological reliability of the personality is a category which reflects social values of the well-rounded personality.

R E F E R E N C E S

1. Nauchno-tekhnicheskaya revolyutsiya i osobennosti sotsial'nogo reazvitiya v sovremennuyu epokhu. Ed., S.I. Nikishov, N.I. Dryakhlov, Izdatel'stvo Moskovskogo universiteta, 1974, Moskva, p. 127.
2. Ibid. p. 129.
3. B.F. Lomov, Chelovek i tekhnika. Leningrad, 1963, p. 7.
4. V.M. Glushkov, Chelovek i vychislitel'naya tekhnika. Kiev, 1971.
5. M. Bobneva, Tekhnika i chelovek. Kommunist, 1964, No. 16. p. 64.
6. G.N. Volkov, Era robotov ili era cheloveka. Moskva, 1965, p. 33.
7. O. Bikkenin, S. Oduyev, Ed., Filosofskaya nauka i ee sovremennye problemy. Kommunist, 1965, No. 5. p. 64.
8. V.B. Biryukov, Filosofskie voprosy kibernetiki. Sbornik statey. Kibernetiku v sluzhbu kommunizmu. Tom 5. Moskva, 1976, p. 305.
9. B.D. Parygin, Sotsial'naya psikhologiya kak nauka. Leningrad, 1968.
10. A.K. Udelov, Ob opredelenii sotsialisticheskikh kollektivov i issledovanii ikh zhizni. Filosofskie nauki, 1968, No. 5.

11. N. Viner, Kibernetika i obshchestvo. Moskva, 1958, p. 31.

12. V.G. Marakhov, Sovremennaya nauchno-tekhnicheskaya revolyutsiya i ee sotsial'niye posledstviya v usloviyakh sotsializma. Voprosy Filosofii, 1966, No. 3. p. 138.

5. THE SOVIET COLLECTIVE, AND PERSONALITY CHARACTERISTICS

In addition to social values of human existence, we must analyze the inner structure of the individual personality structure within collectives. The personality of the contemporary Soviet collective individual is present in his psychological potential and in the general importance of the individual. " Individuality exists in all spheres of intellectual activities: spiritual, emotional, in self-control, in opinions, in political and philosophical views and in individual judgements."(1) The collective aspect and the individual aspect of the personality exist in a dialectical antithesis: they deny each other and they correlate to each other; they form a relationship of mutual elimination and mutual interrelation. The individuality has the characteristics of an independent individual; the collectivity, however, the total number of individuals. " The human being, or individual, takes active part in social planning; however, he is not only an object for the planning system of the society, but rather a subject of the planning process. The process of social planning includes all individuals who have the intention to be useful to the society."(2) Through the realization of principals in planning human existence, individuals are placed into an active relationship with the process of economic planning and its organizational structure. Due to this combination, the process of social planning sets the guidelines and behavior modifications for the socialist society; it helps to develop individual initiative and creative potential which form elements of individuality. " The socialist principles of leadership are not based on manipulation, but on participation of individuals in designing new forecasting and planning systems for the national economy which, on the other hand, requires a maximum of personal initiative and social criticism by individuals. " (3) Socialist social relations are geared toward structural change of the whole social system, including the collective. The interrelationship of various structural models of human relations within the collective form a unified whole which can be described as a collective-individual personality structure. The following structural components form such a unified collective-individual structure of personal and social relations:

1. The structure of functional obligations
2. The structure of economic relations
3. The cadre structure
4. The political, ideological and organizational structure
5. The social-psychological structure

In addition to the structural model of the collective, we have to consider the production efficiency of the collective, the age structure, educational level, cultural activities, as well as its moral and ethical maturity.

Soviet sociological research provides some information concerning the motivation of people to participate and develop social relations and to what extent personal and group stimuli are responsive to social needs and to the general development of a socialist society. The research results show the factors which influence the development of manpower characteristics of collectives in industry and economy. Such factors are:

1. " The growing demands created by the scientific-technological revolution and the intellectual and creative capabilities of individuals within collectives.
2. Individual responsibility within collectives in fulfilling the production plans and the rationalization of special branches of production.
3. Detailed knowledge of economic and scientific-technological problems of the Five-Year-Plan and forecasting models of special production units and branches.
4. A high level of solidarity among workers; furthermore, professional-technical, moral-political and cultural awareness of all individuals.

5. The material interest of individual workers and collectives in accomplishing economic and scientific progress.
6. Cooperation among workers utilizing their individual experience to provide examples of how complex problems of the scientific-technological revolution can be solved, and help to develop individual personality qualities within the collective.
7. An award system for individual workers for their individual and personal accomplishments and for the development of personal qualities.
8. The interest of workers in technological innovations furthers the creative and intellectual caliber of labor.
9. Social relations among small groups of workers; the relationship between the leadership of the collective and individual members of the collective; the relationship between workers and representatives of intellectual elite groups." (4)

The above listed social, political, economic and personal factors come into play daily under certain conditions and to a certain extent, depending on the developmental level of particular collectives. Nevertheless, the above descriptions of manpower developments are only an attempt to systematize the stimuli of collective activities and individual-collective personality formation within activities of collectives.

a. Social-Psychological Relations Within Collectives

The social atmosphere influences the production process of collectives. The social and psychological relations within collectives are structured and divided into:

1. Interpersonal and inter-group relations
2. The relationship between the leadership and their subordinates.
3. Conflict situations
4. The emotional atmosphere

Additional factors which influence social and psychological

relations within the production process of collectives are, " The selection and placement of cadres, the satisfaction derived from work, the degree of realization of goals in life, the degree of satisfaction of value orientations, the organization of leisure time and finally, family relations."(5) The social structure of collectives is also characterized by factors which are related to personality characteristics and behavior models of workers in the Soviet Union. " Competition at work, general management capabilities, social-political work, party work, cultural activities, education, discipline of labor, the accomplishments of work norms, the structure of leisure time, individual consciousness, personal desires, individual preferences, the evaluation of non-collective circumstances through personality characteristics of individuals, satisfaction with professional work performed, general conditions of work and the participation in social work."(6)

The participation of workers in solving practical problems of collectives requires individual responsibility, individual attitudes and individual criticism of members of collectives. The following questionnaire provides information concerning the question: "How do you participate in solving problems within the collective?"

Table XVIII.

INDIVIDUAL MEMBERS OF THE COLLECTIVE PARTICIPATE IN:*

Answers	In % of the total number of questioned
1. The elaboration of production plans	18.5%
2. The revision of the output of collectives	11.9%
3. The distribution of awards and bonuses	37.2%
4. The distribution of travel permits	26.1%
5. The distribution of food	27.3%
6. Hiring and dismissal of workers	31.1%
7. Punishing violations of discipline	49.8%
8. Professional advancement of workers	9.5%
9. The participation in socialist competition	46.3%
10. Did not answer	22.4%

* _Metodika sotsial'nogo planirovaniya kollektiva predpriyatiya._ Perm, 1969, p. 134.

The highest percentage of answers received concerned the violations of discipline within collectives (49.8%). The answers point to a high level of discipline violations, as well as a strong desire of workers to eliminate such human mistakes, which represent a negative aspect of personality formation. It further indicates characteristics of individual personality orientation of workers who criticize such psychological deficiencies within social relations of collectives, and it points to positive personality values as decency, justice and honesty. The second highest percentage of answers was given to the elaboration of socialist competition (46.3%). The distribution of awards and bonuses received (37.2%) of answers which characterize the material and financial concern of workers in relationship to work performed. Hiring and dismissal of workers received (31.1%) of the answers. The distribution of food and the distribution of travel permits received (27.3% and 26.1%) of answers.

The topics listed in the questionnaire represent the daily fundamental needs of Soviet workers. The listed possibilities of participation of workers in active decision-making within collectives give them sufficient independence in determining their individual status within social relations of collectives.

In conclusion, we can identify two trends of personality developments within Soviet collectives. First, the traditional obedience and passivity of the individual personality, due to remoulding and ideological re-education processes. Second, the current social developments and reorganization of the Soviet society strive to increase the output of the national economy and allow workers to develop individual initiatives and independent decision-making within the social processes of collectives. Such initiatives are directed towards the implementation of the scientific-technological revolution and towards establishing a flexible and politically independent management system of production enterprises and collectives. The intentions of the Soviet government in allowing a variety of choices with regard to the decision-making process on all levels of production, indicate the intention to rechannel the political control from strict party obedience to a technocratic-management level of responsible individuals within the Soviet society.

Human values of the collective personality are characterized by adherence to the political cause, and the sincerity of relationships among members of the collective. The psychology of the collective has ' we ' as its starting point and not ' I '. The moral factor in developing the scientific-technological revolution has a strong impact on the formation of collectivity and individuality. Ponomarev analyzed in his book _Stimul material'ny i stimul moral'niy_, various definitions of morality and the practical value of its application within a collective. " The moral encouragement of workers of the collective without sufficient analysis of the moral foundations produces a doubtful glory of ficticious heros and a compromise because of such a moral system of stimulation." (7)

b. Critical Personality Characteristics of Workers Within Collectives

The questionnaire study, conducted at the Irkutsk region, describes the personality characteristics of workers of the aluminium factory Shelekhove. The majority of questioned workers criticize the effectiveness in solving complex problems of collectives. The answers indicate the indifference of workers toward various forms of mass participation in social relations, as well as labor relations, within collectives. (Table XIX.)

Table XIX.

CRITICAL PERSONALITY CHARACTERISTICS OF WORKERS*

Answers	In % of the total number of questioned
1. Indifference toward professional performance	14.3%
2. The work in the collective is performed without enthusiasm	11.7%
3. Confused methods of instruction	7.4%
4. Ineffective political training	7.3%
5. Matters not related to the collective	3.3%
6. Problems within the collective are solved superficially	6.8%

*_Lichnost' i kollektiv_. Irkutsk, 1973, p. 129.

The critical evaluation of social conditions as well as of working conditions within the aluminium factory Shelekhove of the Irkutsk region again reaffirms the theory of social criticism and individual initiative within the contemporary Soviet society.

Indifference toward professional performance (14.3%) and work performed without enthusiasm (11.7%) shows the absence of enthusiasm with regard to increasing the production process and the efficiency of the collective. Confused educational methods as well as an ineffective political organization of workers (7.4% and 7.3%) reflect critical attitudes about ideological participation in collectives. (6.8%) of workers said that problems within the collective are solved superficially. Such opinions refer directly to poor leadership capabilities within the production enterprise Shelekhove.

R E F E R E N C E S

1. Kollektiv i lichnost'. Akademiya obshchestvennykh nauk pri TsK KPSS, Kafedra Filosofii, Izdatel'stvo " Mysl' ", Moskva, 1968, p. 52.
2. Ibid. p. 54.
3. Ibid. p. 67.
4. Ibid. p. 113.
5. Kollektiv i lichnost'. Ed., G.I. Mel'nikov, V.N. Sudakov, Ministerstvo vysshego i srednego spetsial'nogo obrazovaniya RSFSR, Irkutskiy gosudarstvennyy universitet imeni A.A. Zhdanova, Irkutsk, 1972, p. 33.
6. Metodika sotsial'nogo planirovaniya kollektiva predpriyatiya. Perm, 1969, p. 21.
7. Ponomarev, Stimul material'ny i stimul moral'niy. Alma-Ata, 1965, p. 70.

6. LEADERSHIP QUALITIES AND PERSONALITY CHARACTERISTICS OF SOVIET MANAGERS, PARTY OFFICIALS, TEACHERS AND ENGINEERS

The training of leadership cadres on an advanced level is being undertaken at special educational institutions, and management schools, which adopted the training program of the Advanced Party School and the Academy of General Sciences at the Central Committee of the CPSU where Party leaders are trained.

Additional leadership training centers and institutions are, The Institute for Management of the National Economy with 50 branches of federal and affiliated republican institutes for professional advancement, as well as 70 subdivisions of these institutes; 93 special university courses are being offered; 11 faculty level training programs on the organization of industrial production and construction are being offered; 600 permanent courses are being offered at enterprises, organizations and other institutions. The Advanced School for Agricultural Management, in Moscow, is attached to the Ministry of Agriculture of the USSR, as well as for managing provincial, regional and autonomous Republics of the USSR.

The methodological basis for the study of leadership in the USSR is dialectical and historical materialism, which is viewed as the interaction of people and social groups. Such societal interactions are influenced by the character of the group, the sphere of its activity, the psychological makeup of the participants, the direction and purpose of activities, and the personality of the leader. Leadership develops as an objective need of the group, which is transformed in the consciousness of individual members of the collective and takes the form of demands and expectations directed toward the individual who is playing the role of the leader.

Various sciences study leadership in the Soviet Union. Psychology and psychiatry investigate the personality characteristics of leaders, whereas sociology examines leadership from the perspective of a social system. Social psychology studies leadership as the interaction of social and psychological factors, investigates its mechanism, and develops methods for the selection, instruction, and promotion of leaders. The problem of political leadership is particularly important. Marxist researchers rely on the theory of relations between masses, classes, parties and political leaders as formulated by Lenin: " Political leadership develops during the class struggle."(1) " Not a single class in history has achieved power without producing its political leaders, its prominent representatives, who are able to organize a movement and lead it."(2)

The utilization of the cadres is the major instrument of the party leadership to manage Soviet society. In formulating this policy, the leadership is continually attempting to reconcile two partially contradictory criteria: loyalty to the party's goals and professional ability. The leadership of the Soviet communist party has been able to accomplish this task, while retaining strict political control. However, since Khrushchev's fall there have been growing signs that a weakening central direction plus an increased demand for expertise in managerial positions has led to an increase of the operational independence of cadres. The current prospects for centralized administration of cadres affairs depend on the Soviet leadership's ability to make the necessary concession to the requirements of managerial efficiency without fatally weakening the foundations of its own political power.

Many managers of Soviet production enterprises are still not able to develop individual initiative in connection with leadership capabilities within their collectives. These managers do not think independently and they are unable to foresee and solve complex problems of the production process. They also do not consult co-workers of the collective on matters related to the improvement of production. Furthermore, the managers neglect their professional improvement and advancement. The absence of human concern and a lack of a strong leadership negatively influence the general atmosphere of the collective. The described managerial deficiencies point to the absence of leadership qualities and characterize these people as poor administrators.

The following is the order of professional qualifications and personality characteristics of managers, as required by official Soviet party guidelines:

1. " Ideological priorities for the leadership cadres;
2. Frequent participation at seminars of management techniques and the art of leadership;

3. The specialist-managers should be educated in economic matters, in contemporary methods of calculation and in all aspects of cybernetics." (3)

Leadership combines the process of organization and management, which is performed jointly by all members of the collective. The leader or manager should be only an intermediator and regulator of social control and the power of the decision-making processes within collectives. " The leadership is a process of inner-psychological organization and management of collectives. The leadership requires harmony between activities and the behavior of people in improving social norms and applying moral principles within society." (4)

A.A. Yershov, a psychologist from Leningrad, established the theory that the effectiveness of leadership depends on the intensity of the leader's authority. S.E. Kamenitser pointed out that leadership qualities of managers require higher professional performance on the part of the staff, greater work effectiveness, and a progressive and optimal approach to all decisions that have to be worked out. In order to make the administrative work less time consuming, the management is backed up by modern organizational and computer technology.

There are different options for improving the management system and the efficiency of leadership of production enterprises. A management type of personality structure is characterized by the ability to organize labor relations which are based on scientific knowledge and advanced technological systems. " A manager has to be able to conduct fair placement policies and has to rationalize the use of manpower. The distribution of wages should be based on accomplishments and merits and not on privileges. The leadership personality has to be flexible and independent in the decision-making processes which pertain to particular collectives. In addition, the selection process for leadership positions has to be constantly improved."(5)

S.V. Nevmerzhitskiy presented in his article, Kachestva rukovoditelya i nravstvennye otnosheniya v proizvodstvennom kollektive, (Leadership Qualities and Moral Relations within a Production Enterprise), the view, that " Members of collectives should not be treated by their leadership only as manpower, but as colleagues and friends, as individual personalities. The leader must possess strong volitional qualities, which should be used in connection with ' power '. The leader should not only admire and respect his own personality, but also the personality of all members of the collective."(6)

a. The Social and Psychological Characteristics of Leadership Roles

The leading contemporary Soviet social scientists, E.S. Kuz'min, I.P. Volkov, Yu.N. Emel'yanov, (Rukovoditel' i kolektiv; Leadership and Collective), A.G. Kovalev, (Kollektiv i sotsial'no-psikhologicheskie problemy rukovodstva; The Collective and Social-Psychological Problems of Leadership), I.S. Mangutov, L.I. Umanskiy, (Organizator i organizatorskaya deyatel'nost'; The Organizer and Organizational Activities), have evaluated the leadership qualities within Soviet production enterprises in their latest publications.

The leadership qualities of managers of Soviet production enterprises can be divided into two aspects: 1. Production related technological activities and 2. Social-psychological activities. In connection with the production related technological function, the manager (leader) of the production enterprise fullfils the function as a specialist of the production process. Such managerial activities do not differ from the professional performance of engineers and technical personnel. The leadership of production enterprises deal with people and therefore presupposes the presence of social-psychological functions.

The structure of social-psychological functions of leadership activities is divided into four groups: 1. Informational, 2. Organizational, 3. Socializational, 4. Decision-making function. The informational function is characterized by gathering information and reporting different information for the regulation of group processes. The informational function also appears in the regulation between the production related communication and personal information, which relates the manager of the production enterprise with his staff. The organization is the essential and most responsible role of managers. The organizational role of managers is divided in: 1. Planning and disseminating information among the staff. 2. The interpretation of concrete tasks of the staff belongs to the control exponent of the organizational ability of managers. The manager is obligated to control the time schedule of work; in addition, he controls the discipline and quality of work. The control function is divided with regard to the quality of the control function. Due to the constant control of workers activities, the manager has the opportunity to assist his staff at the same time. The awards for factory workers and organizers of production are moral recognition and material improvements. The reprimands and punishments are made possible by strict supervision of all activities of particular workers involved.

The four stages of the leadership process appear united in one person who performs the organizational function and represents conscious, goal-oriented and diverse activities of the manager, who directs and coordinates the performance of workers. The organizational functions of managers include the protection of workers' interests with regard to higher placed organizations; the improvement of production conditions and the coordination of work of production units; the education of workers personality.

The manager also makes the necessary decisions with regard to production related activities as well as with regard to personal matters of workers. The manager can make the decisions in two ways: 1. To consult his staff and assistants; 2. To make decisions independently. The first way of managerial decision-making is typical for the democratic process of work, since it fulfills the social-psychological responsibilities. The second way represents authoritarian leadership characteristics. (See Table XX.)

b. Leadership Characteristics and Personality Qualities of Managers

The description of leadership characteristics and elite group attitudes, in relationship to subordinates of collectives, provides insight into the general psychological structures and behavioral attitudes of workers. (Table XX.) The realtionship between individuality and collectivity and

Table XX.

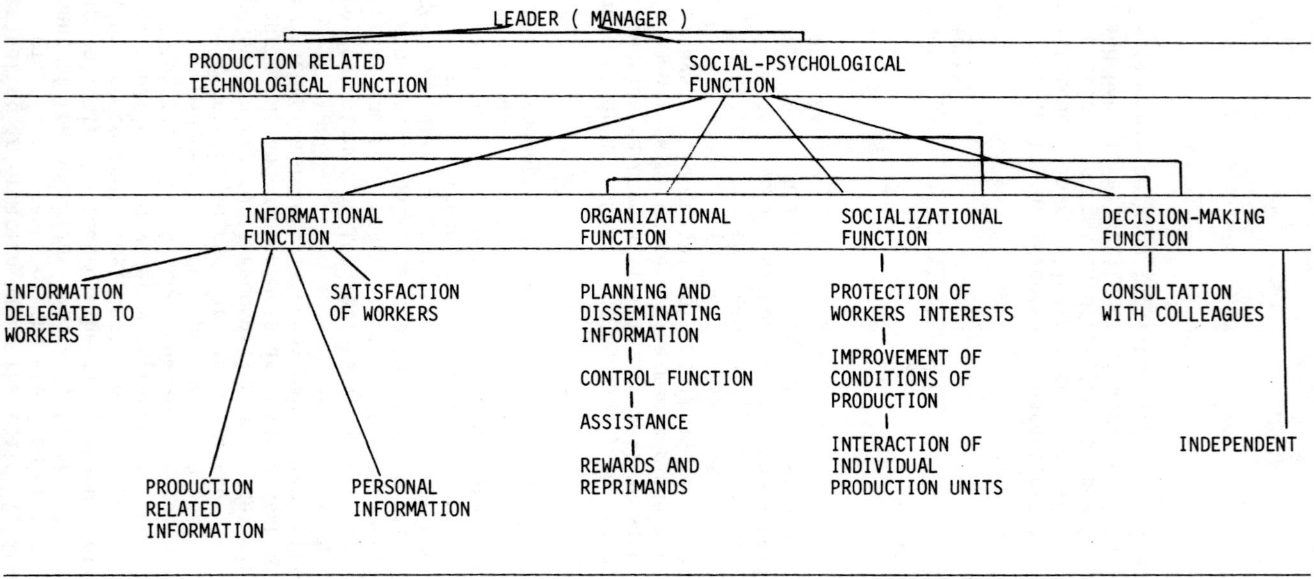

THE STRUCTURE OF LEADERSHIP ACTIVITIES WITHIN PRODUCTION ENTERPRISES IN THE USSR

personality development is determined by the decision-making process of the management and leadership of production enterprises. The leadership of collectives must possess special knowledge about social processes, specifically about their control mechanism, about the psycho-physiological and socially preconditioned qualities of their subordinates. The knowledge of social characteristics is necessary for the realization of the interests of workers and for the coordination of their material needs: wages, living conditions, their social advancement, work performance, the authority structure of collectives and inter-personal relations among workers of collectives.
Two general types of leadership personalities of managers of collectives are analyzed by Soviet sociologists: 1. The candidate should be selected to leadership positions because of objective personality characteristics, which means, people who will guarantee equal chances for all, and 2. those, who share the advantages of the production process with the workers of collectives.

Table XXI.

MORAL QUALITIES OF LEADERS (MANAGERS) OF PRODUCTION ENTERPRISES EVALUATED BY THEIR STAFF*

Moral Qualities	% of affirmative answers
1. He must possess a sense of duty and responsibility	76
2. He must be polite	72
3. He must be modest	71
4. He must adhere to principles	66
5. He must be honest and possess integrity	65

* V.A. Osetrov, _Vliyanie vzaimootnoshenii rukovoditelya i podchinennogo na upravlenie proizvodstvennym kollektivom._ In: Lichnost' i kollektiv. Ministerstvo srednego i vysshego spetsial'nogo obrazovania RSFSR. Irkutskiy gosudarstvennyy universitet, Irkutsk, 1973, p. 37.

Table XXII.

ORGANIZATIONAL QUALITIES OF LEADERS (MANAGERS) OF PRODUCTION ENTERPRISES EVALUATED BY THEIR STAFF *

Organizational Qualities	% of affirmative answers
1. He must be demanding	76
2. He must be able to explain his thoughts	75
3. He must be able to influence his subordinates	69
4. He must be able to develop initiatives	62
5. He must be able to develop proper perspectives for his work	61
6. He must be respected as an authority by his subordinates	59
7. He must be able to promote qualified workers	51
8. He must be able to teach his subordinates to be independent	42
9. He must have a strong determination	39

* V.A. Osetrov, Vliyanie vzaimootnoshenii rukovoditelya i podchinennogo na upravlenie proizvodstvennym kollektivom. In: Lichnost' i kollektiv. Ministerstvo srednego i vysshego spetsial'nogo obrazovaniya RSFSR. Irkutskiy gosudarstvennyy universitet i, A.A. Zhdanova, Irkutsk, 1973, p. 38.

Table XXIII.

PROFESSIONAL QUALITIES OF LEADERS (MANAGERS) OF PRODUCTION ENTERPRISES EVALUATED BY THEIR STAFF*

Professional Qualities	% of affirmative answers
1. He is an asset to technological progress	72
2. He must be knowledgeable about technical and economic processes	64
3. He must be able to organize sales and supply	59
4. He must have knowledge of work procedures and labor relations	58
5. He must be able to apply scientific principles of management	53
6. He must be able to communicate with other section chiefs of enterprises	51
7. He must understand the systems approach within the management structure	46

*V.A. Osetrov, Vliyanie vzaimootnoshenii rukovoditelya i podchinennogo na upravlenie proizvodstvennym kollektivom. In: Lichnost' i kollektiv. Ministerstvo srednego i vysshego spetsial'nogo obrazovaniya RSFSR. Irkutskiy gosudarstvennyy universitet im. A.A. Zhdanova, Irkutsk, 1973, p. 41.

Table XXIV.

HUMAN QUALITIES OF LEADERS (MANAGERS) OF PRODUCTION ENTERPRISES EVALUATED BY THEIR STAFF *

Human Qualities	% of affirmative answers
1. He should help his subordinates	75
2. He should be responsive	74
3. He should be able to understand the problems of his subordinates	72
4. He should maintain a good relationship with his subordinates	62
5. He should maintain a non-authoritative relationship with his subordinates	63
6. He should have a good sense of humor	47
7. He should be able to accept criticism	45
8. He should be objective towards people criticizing him	36
9. He should not impose or dictate his working style to his subordinates	33

* V.A. Osetrov, Vliyanie vzaimootnoshenii rukovoditelya i podchinennogo na upravlenie proizvodstvennym kollektivom. In: Lichnost' i kollektiv. Ministerstvo srednego i vysshego spetsial'nogo obrazovaniya RSFSR. Irkutskiy gosudarstvennyy universitet im. A.A. Zhdanova, Irkutsk, 1973, p. 43.

The analysis of Tables XX. through XXIV. indicates that the management qualities and personality characteristics of leaders of production enterprises consist of different types of managerial abilities: Moral qualities, organizational qualities, professional qualities, and human qualities. The manager must know the sector he manages, its machinery, technology, and organization. He must be able to organize a collective and make each worker an active participant in the fulfillment of the set task. He must have knowledge of economics, law, sociology, and psychology. In addition, the manager is assisted by a large number of specialists, who help him to provide the necessary leadership.

On the other hand, one-man management includes the use of many possible methods of management: 1. Organizational methods, which consist of the selection and disposition of personnel, the determination of the efficient organization of the sector being managed and the managing agencies, as well as the establishment of a clear scope of work, rights, and responsibilities of each subdividion and manager; 2. Economic methods, which make use of the worker's personal interests in improving production efficiency as well as of the relationship between the worker's material prosperity and the result of the activity of the group as a whole; 3. Educational methods, directed towards increasing the production activity of workers and towards the development of their sense of responsibility and initiative.

c. Leadership Qualities and Personality Characteristics of Soviet Party Officials

Soviet sociological surveys illustrate the re-orientation of Soviet citizen in social participation. The individual is becoming a thinking human being with the opportunity of free choice with regard to personal desires. This new individualistic character carries the potential of self-determination and responsibility which has not been allowed within the Soviet society under traditional party rule and control. The developmental stage of a new personality within contemporary Soviet social relations however, creates a conflict situation with regard to the collective activities of the individual and the individual initiative within the social process. Individual initiative is strongly emphasized by the decree of the Presidio of the Supreme Soviet of the USSR with regard to activities and behavior guidelines for delegates of the Supreme Soviet of the USSR.

The subjective factor of delegates is recommended for the decision-making process on all levels of party activities. Only an active participation of the delegates, on the basis of personal innovation and initiative, in the society can serve as an educative tool and influence the mass character of the whole society. " The Soviet delegate does not issue party directives; he is supposed to teach the masses and to learn from the masses. A succesful educational activity can be accomplished only by a delegate through his personal approach and his individual example - in fulfilling his duty as a representative of the electorate."(7) " The delegate must have the following qualifications: He must be respectful, authoritative, a good organizer; he should possess a warm human culture, realistic life experience, the basic knowledge of human psychology, and he must be able to approach each individual as an individual. The personality qualifications and human culture are obtained by direct contact with the electorate and through the exchange of political and social views."(8)

Party members at the highest level of the leadership structure must receive professional training at one of the Party Schools of the Central Committee of the CPSU which are part of the Academy of the Social Sciences of the Central Committee of the CPSU, in one of the following disciplines: " Party History, Party Structure, Theory and Methods of Ideological Work, Foreign Political Propaganda, Philosophy, Scientific Communism, Political Economy, International Workers Movement, Government and Legal Theories, Soviet History, Literary Theory and Literary Criticism, Art Theory and Scientific Communism."(9)

d. Personality Characteristics of Soviet Educators

Soviet education is a powerful factor in personality development. By providing a general education and equipping students with knowledge about nature, society and thought, as well as with work habits and skills, the Soviet schools form communist convictions, communist world views and communist moral and volitional qualities in young people. At the same time, training of the personality promotes the successful acquisition of knowledge. The unity of education, study, and upbringing is achieved by putting into practice the principle of study that disciplines the individual. It further includes the work of upbringing and personality development in the system of extracurricular activities provided by the Pioneer and Komsomol organizations.

There are, according to Anweiler, three types of models useful in explaining the communist educational system:" Models dealing with the relationship between education and society; 2. Models describing the functions of the educational system; 3. Models relating education to training and learning. The last model endeavors to ascertain the contribution of education to personality development."(10)

A Soviet educator must possess qualifications which characterize his teaching abilities, as well as his intellectual personality qualities.

Table XXV.

PROFESSIONAL QUALIFICATIONS OF SOVIET EDUCATORS*

1. Logical interpretation of school texts as they relate to real facts.
2. The ability to analyze and compare.
3. Independent formulation of questions with regard to teaching new materials.
4. The ability to conduct basic research.
5. The ability to make independent conclusions.
6. The ability to solve problems as they relate to social activities.
7. The ability to assist weak students.
8. The ability to use traditional means in influencing the activities of students.

---

* N.A. Mednikova, Ispol'zovanie dostizhenii pedagogiki i pedagogicheskoy psikhologii rukovoditelem shkoly v analize uchebno-vospitatel'nogo protsessa. In: Psikhologiya - proisvodstva i vospitaniya. Izdatel'stvo Leningradskogo universiteta, Leningrad, 1977, p. 207. Ed., A.A. Krylov.

Table XXVI.

LEADERSHIP QUALITIES AND PERSONALITY CHARACTERISTICS OF EDUCATORS EVALUATED BY STUDENTS*

Qualities	No. of answers	%	with degree	without d.
1. Is an authority in the field	189	18.7	66	123
2. Proved himself as an instructor	237	23.5	76	161
3. A good worker, but without knowledge of people	106	10.5	16	90
4. Knowledge of people, but not a good instructor	44	4.4	9	35
5. He combines persistence and demands with the sensitivity to understand people	228	22.6	71	157
6. Demanding, but does not care about difficulties at work	116	11.5	21	95
7. Gives priorities to research and little attention to educational and methodological work	46	4.5	21	25
8. Strongly emphasizes educational work and gives little attention to research	43	4.3	15	28
Total answers	1009	100	295	714

* L.N. Litvinov, _Trud i byt kak faktory formirovaniya lichnosti_. Priokskoe knizhnoe izdatel'stvo, Tula, 1973, p. 149.

Leadership qualities and personality characteristics of educators are divided as follows with regard to the preference of students (Table XXVI.). 189 students or 18.7% of all answers preferred a teacher who is an authority in his field. However, only 66 students with advanced degrees accepted a teacher as an authority in his field as compared to 123 students without an advanced degree. 237 students approved a teacher who was a good instructor or 25.5% of all questioned students, which seems to be the first priority of personality qualities of educators in the capacity as an intellectual or spiritual leader of young people. To be a good worker without the knowledge of the psychology of people is more important to students than a teacher who is able to communicate satisfactorly with people, but who is not a good instructor. Only 44 students answered affirmatively to such personality qualities, which represents the lowest percentage of all answers. However, a teacher who is able to combine persistence and academic demands with the sensitivity of people, received a total of 228 or 22.6% of all answers. The importance in given preference to research activities rather than to educational or methodological work is similar to the preference for educational excellence, 46 to 43 students to 4.5% to 4.3% of all answers.

e. Leadership Qualities and Personality Characteristics of Engineers and Technical Personnel

The policy of the CPSU and the Soviet government with regard to cadres is aimed at promoting talented, politically conscious, educated and professionally trained personnel. The CPSU considers it necessary "... to constantly extend and improve the system of training and re-training cadres - the organizers of production at all levels, including the highest leadership cadres, particularly in the fields of Marxist-Leninist economic theory, the theories and practices of management, the scientific organization of labor and new methods of planning, economic incentives and modern computer technology."(11)

Great demands are made of the leadership cadres, who are expected to have a mastery of modern managerial methods, a feeling for new developments and their long-term prospects, an ability to use the most efficient means of problem-solving and to draw on the knowledge and experience of others. In February of 1971, the Institute for the Management of the National Economy opened in Moscow. The institute perfects the training of leadership cadres, including ministers in industry and economy. A further means for training cadres and improving their work is self-criticism and criticism, particularly from below. A resolution of the 24th Congress of the CPSU specifies, " We must raise the cadres' sense of responsibility in regard to tasks assigned to them and take the necessary measures with regard to those who violate discipline, who do not draw the necessary conclusions from criticism, and who conduct themself incorrectly."

The recent accomplishments of scientific institutions and of scientific research have given rise to numerous new definitions of the concept of scientific activity. One of the definitions of scientific activity is provided in the study: The Revolution in Science and Engineering and the Change in the Structure of Scientific Personnel in the USSR " Work is directed towards gaining new knowledge of the laws of development of nature and society, of the fundamental properties of engineering systems, towards investigation of the direction to be taken in using scientific knowledge in production, and the development on this basis, of new engineering designs, technological processes, and the verification of their effectiveness."(12)

The activities of scientific personnel constitutes a system that has its own structure, its own inner links, and its own development. We identify the following structural activities of scientific personnel: the design of future research directions; the collection of scientific data; the analysis of scientific information and compilation of surveys; the development of working hypotheses and research techniques; experimental work; analysis of research results; writing of research reports. All these structural elements of activities of scientific personnel require different approaches to the respective goals and presuppose the existence of special knowledge and professional expertise.

The increase of the scope of science is occuring under the conditions of improvement in the organization of the labor force and management, the introduction of new technology, computers, etc. The following aspects of scientific activities are typical features of change within contemporary Soviet science policy:

1. " The increasing technical sophistication of contemporary research.
2. The increasing complexity of organization of research.
3. The broader use of experimental methods, modeling, and mathematical methods of research.
4. The process of differentiation in science, and simultaneously its increasing integration and the appearance of a unified system of scientific knowledge.
5. The appearance and development of information theories as a new science, and the use of its methods in many spheres of scientific research."(13)

f. Scientific Personnel and Social Classes

Scientific personnel comprise a significant proportion of the intelligentsia in the USSR. However, different views exist with regard to the place of the intelligentsia in the class structure of the Soviet society. D.V. Arutyunyan characterizes the intelligentsia as an independent social structure, while others, K.I. Mamayeva, regard it as a social group. Some Soviet authors recognize nothing distinctive in the intelligentsia to make it an independent structure, and they categorize it as part of the working class or part of the social stratum of white collar people. Yu. A. Kurnosov, for example, in his *K voprosu ob opredelenii ponyatiya ' intelligentsiya ' v sotsialisticheskom obshchestve*, (The Definition of the Term ' Intelligentsia ' within the Socialist Society), regards the intelligentsia as consisting of people with high cultural and ethical standards, equipped with the Marxist world view. An intermediate position is taken by scholars who regard the intelligentsia as a separate social stratum.

The need to improve the structure of scientific cadres under the conditions of the revolution in science and technology has been pointed out in a number of decrees by Party and government: " On Measures to Further Improve Selection and Training of Scientific Cadres " (1962); " On Measures to Improve the Training of Professionals and Paraprofessionals and the Administration of Higher and Specialized Secondary Education in the Country " (1966); " On Improving the Training of Scientific Research and Scientific Education of Cadres " (1967); " On the 250th Anniversary of the USSR Academy of Sciences " (1975);"(14)

The creative activities of engineers and technical personnel are characterized by different levels of professional performance: 1. Inventive thinking; 2. Scientific creativity; 3. Contribution to the creative performance of collectives.

Specific personality characteristics are connected with creative activities of engineers. The intellect of engineers includes, in addition to the general erudition, logical thinking capabilities. The practical intellect is interrelated with the verbal intellect, which means that the level of practical professional knowledge and creative activities depends on the general erudition of the personality of engineers. Engineers with different seniority status, as well as novices, might demonstrate highly developed intellectual qualities within their professional and technical performance. On the other hand, the psychological characteristics of individual engineers, who hold high administrative positions, appear less professional in their performance than engineers with highly qualified professional performance, who do not hold high administrative or professional positions.

The inter-personal relations and personality qualities of leaders of scientific institutions should be able to equalize their professional standards with their social obligation. " A leader must possess qualities, both professional and personal, which equal ' a generator of ideas '. A leader must further be able to communicate with his subordinates and must recognize good performance of work, and must have a personal interest in work procedures; he must be further able to transmit such abilities to his co-workers and develop individual initiatives in solving technical problems and scientific tasks." (15)

The aspiration of leadership and authority among technical

Table XXVII.

WHAT CHARACTER TRAITS SHOULD A WORKER, FOREMAN AND ENGINEER POSSESS?*

Personality Qualities

	In % of the total number of questioned			
	Worker	Foremen	Engineer	Total
1. Ideological firmness, political maturity, moral stability, integrity, adherence to principles	14	13	15	14
2. Justice, intelligence, politeness	17	22	22	21
3. Technical competence, personal culture	24	18	12	18
4. Organizational ability, psychological ability to understand people	12	13	14	13
5. Resouceful, disciplined, vigorous, persistent	8	9	9	9
6. Demanding with people	14	16	16	15
7. Demanding with one-self	6	4	5	5
8. Other qualities	3	6	7	5

* K.K. Platonov, Ed., Lichnost' i trud. Izdatel'stvo " Mysl' ", Moskva, 1965, p. 305.

personnel and engineers appears as a personality characteristic of individuals who are capable of solving complicated technical problems require a highly developed sense of responsibility. (Table XXVII.) provides a more detailed analysis with regard to the question: " What character traits should a worker, foreman and an engineer possess?"

The answers give us a psychological picture of professional abilities and personality characteristics of the three professional groups. The answers are divided into various groups of personality characteristics. In the first group, one finds the moral orientation of the personality of technical specialists. Moral stability, ideological firmness, integrity, adherence to principles received an average of 14% of affirmative answers. Justice and intelligence are significantly higher with an average of 21%. The second group of personality qualities combines technical competence with the organizational ability of professional workers, which received an average of 18% and 13% affirmative answers. The third group of personality qualities includes will-power characteristics. The average figure for positive character traits is 9%, 15%, 5% for all three groups of professional performance.

REFERENCES

1. V.I. Lenin, Poln.sobr. soch. 5th ed., Vol. 41. p. 24.
2. Ibid. Vol. 4. p. 375.
3. V.A. Gorshkov, Puti povisheniya tvorcheskoy initsiativy i aktivnosti narodnykh mass. Ministerstvo vysshego i srednego spetsial'nogo obrazovaniya RSFSR, Povolzhskiy lesotekhnicheskiy institut imeni M. Gor'kogo. Mariyskoe knizhnoe izdatel'stvo, Yoshkar-Ola, 1967.
4. Sotsial'naya psikhologiya lichnosti. Ed., Semenov, Leningrad, 1974, p. 79.
5. V.A. Gorshkov, p. 29.
6. Filosofskie problemy obshchestvennogo razvitiya. Ed., A.G. Kharchev, Akademiya obshchestvennykh nauk pri TsK KPSS, Kafedra marksistko-leninskoy filosofii. Izdatel'stvo " Mysl' ", Moskva, 1975, p. 97.
7. Vedomosti Verkhovnogo Soveta SSSR. No.17.(1415), p. 144.

8. D.D. Ryabov, Sotsialisticheskoe gosudarstvo i vospitanie novogo cheloveka. Izdatel'stvo Moskovskogo universiteta, 1972, pp. 189-190.
9. Georg Brunner, Politische Soziologie der UDSSR. Teil I. Akademische Verlagsgesellschaft Wiesbaden, 1977, p. 78.
10. B. Harasymiw, Education and the Mass Media in the Soviet Union and Eastern Europe. Praeger, New York, p. 11.
11. Materialy XXIV s'ezda KPSS, Moskva, 1971, p. 298.
12. Nauchno-tekhnicheskaya revolyutsiya i izmenenie struktury nauchnikh kadrov SSSR. Moskva, 1973, pp. 30-31.
13. I.S. Puchkov, G.A. Popov, Sotsial'no-demograficheskaya kharakteristika nauchnikh kadrov. Statistika Izdatel'-stvo, Moskva, 1976.
14. KPSS v rezolyutsiyakh i resheniyakh s'ezdov, konferentsii i plenumov TsK. Moskva, Vol. 9., 1966-1968. pp. 125-135.
15. M.Ya., Korneyev, Problemy sotsial'noy tipologii lichnosti. Izdatel'stvo Leningradskogo universiteta, 1971, p. 74.

S U M M A R Y

The development of Soviet psychology of personality during the early 1920's and 1930's was strongly influenced by pedagogical concepts of N.K. Krupskaya, who developed basic principles of the new psychological school which would ensure unimpeded development of personality. Outlining her psychological approach by individual characteristics, she emphasized that the child is a ' living human personality without complex inner life.' However, the entire initial period after the October Revolution has the imprint of new Soviet psychology struggling with the idealist psychology. Therefore, Soviet psychologists relied in many aspects on the research of foreign scholars. Beginning in about the mid 1940's, A.G. Kovalev analyzed personality qualities which determine undesirable behavior in the schoolchild (shyness, impulsiveness, coarseness). However, it was only gradually that Soviet psychologists began to relate questions of the formation of moral consciousness and behavior to questions of the formation of the moral-psychological qualities of the child's personality.

In the early 1950's, the formation of different character traits was analyzed within the psychology of the Soviet personality, as for example, susceptibility to discipline, self-confidence, and sense of responsibility. A.G. Kovalev and V.I. Selivanov have written doctoral theses on the development of volitional personality traits; studies of the role of society in the formation of personality have continued, but Soviet psychologists had not yet reached a decisive turning point in the study of personality, especially with regard to the formation of the character and moral qualities of Soviet man.

Isolated studies have outlined that which is formed under the influence of the collective without illuminating how personality is formed, the forms of social influence, and how the collective itself develops. Soviet psychologists and philosophers have been critical of the view that certain developments in human society, like industrialization or automation, result in the appearance of certain feelings, notably that of alienation. (Krylov, 1964, Bueva, 1965). Soviet psychologists have made a strong argument for the concrete study of individual personality. Many writers urge a move away from abstract formulations, which were merely a restatement of the principle of dialectical materialism applied to society and the individual. Such views appear as opposing the dogma that only class psychology exists.

The present concept of Soviet personality is defined by the direct participation in social activity. Georgi Smirnov emphasizes individual personality characteristics and unique qualities of individuals and originality of thought. The guidelines of the Communist Party of the USSR are contrary to the previous concept concerning contemporary development and importance of the personality traits. The personality of Soviet man, states the Program of the CPSU, is effected by participation in building communism and the development of communist principles in the economic and social spheres. Through systematic research of personal and intellectual value orientation, the Soviet Communist Party leadership becomes directly involved in shaping the personal values of Soviet citizens.

The Soviet human value system exists in individual and collective motivation, and political activism in connection with developing and applying the principles of the scientific-technological revolution. Man is the central problem of Marxist-

Leninist philosophy, psychology, sociology, law, biology, medicine and art.

Contemporary Soviet social scientists divided the concept of the personality into a progressive and ideal personality. The personality qualities as spiritual and creative qualities of individuals, the deepening of emotions and feelings, freedom of the personality and the development of self-awareness are major factors within current research on personality models and structure (A.I. Tatarenko). Additional personality concepts are characterized by scientific and professional knowledge, and mutual respect within the family (D.D. Ryabov).

The traditional Soviet concept of personality characteristics of an ideal man is illustrated by the following human qualities: Love for the Soviet Union, subordination of personal emotions, needs, values to that of the Party, patriotism, solidarity; the ideal Soviet man is anti-individualistic as well as atheistic. The traditional Soviet personality models are based on the ideological principles exemplified and decreed by the Central Committee during the Lenin, Stalin and Khrushchev eras. These personality characteristics reflect totalitarian value orientations. Thus, the interpretation of Soviet personality structures by American scholars have been portrayed correctly in describing it as a functioning attitude of individuals under totalitarian control mechanisms and totalitarian value perceptions.

Patriotism, atheism, and collectivism on the other hand, are slogans which have been used by Mao Tse-tung in the early period of the People's Republic of China. Such personality values have been directly adopted from Stalinist ideological concepts and transplanted into the Chinese Communist mass-campaign of re-education and remoulding.

The history and development of the Soviet personality structure goes back to the October Revolution of 1917. V.I. Lenin formulated the ideological concepts of the human value system as part of the Marxist-Leninist ideological doctrine. This concept was modified by Stalin, and transformed into an official control mechanism of human values, which manipulated the behavior of Soviet citizens. The Stalinist totalitarian guidelines for personality structures were applied within the

Soviet society until the 23rd Party Congress of the CPSU in 1966. The Central Committee of the CPSU introduced in August 1967 the resolution " On Measures for Further Developing the Social Sciences and Strengthening Their Role in Communist Construction." This resolution gave the Soviet social scientists more leeway in developing new scientific approaches and research methods in forming a contemporary human value system, which is seen as a result of the scientific-technological revolution.

The re-orientation process of the Soviet social sciences is primarily concerned with management capabilities of individuals, as well as individual responsibility, instead of the traditional communist ideological guidelines within the formation process of personality models.

The personality is seen by Soviet psychologists as the apex of the mental process of man, since it represents the highest level of self-orientation and self-guidance. Soviet psychology of the personality analyzes extensively the concept of the will in relationship to personality formation and behavior modification. The volitional qualities of the personality are the creation of original capabilities of man in solving obstacles during the realization of goals. Further personality types within Soviet psychology include a progressive personality and an ideological personality. The ideological personality accomplishes a maximum development of individual capabilities in connection with social changes and in overcoming alienation.

The central value center of human existence is connected with the personality structure. This center determines the values of life and its self-conduct. Within the Marxist theory, the value orientation has the regulatory function of the personality with regard to social values (Yu.V. Sychev).

Marxist sociology of the personality does research on many different levels, including changes in the social types of the personality, and the correlation among autonomous factors in the socialization of the personality in the organization. It further investigates the social interaction of individuals in different social groups and needs. However, the development of creative activity of each individual is the most important prerequisite for the shaping of the new personality within Soviet sociology (I. Kon).

The concept of the personality in Soviet art is seen as a creative form, as a carrier of material and spiritual values. Personality traits appear as creative stimuli which define the individual participation in cultural life. The artist is therefore interested in specific and general peculiarities of the personality.

Aesthetics has the obligation to reunite the theoretical and historical aspect of the ' art of personality '. The didactic-materialistic concept of the personality and society is the social image of the personality; it is expressed through the personality of the artist (Kagan). Kagan relates the personality concept to artistic creativity in saying that the personality as a subject of creative activities questions the performance of the personality of artists within art history; that the personality is an object of artistic figurative cognition; and that personality as a subject of artistic perception includes the formation process of the personality and its aesthetic education.

N.S. Khrushchev pointed out at the 21st Party Congress, that the role of writers and artists is "... selecting the best sentiments and qualities of man, disclosing to him his tomorrow."

The Soviet interpretation of freedom of the personality is based on an analysis of the subject of personality. Freedom of the personality has different interpretative variations, for example, economic freedom of the personality, spiritual freedom of the personality, and political freedom of the personality. Freedom of the personality can be further defined as freedom of family life, freedom of personal aspirations. The practical realization of freedom of the personality depends on the level of realization of objective conditions within a society. Borovskiy defines freedom of the personality in saying that " Determinism is characterized mainly by the perception and the emotions of infra-personal and moral-psychological freedom of the personality which enables the subject through the process of motivation to obtain its choice and to achieve its accepted purpose."

The expansion of the freedom of the personality depends on the growth of the personality. Responsibility is possible only under conditions of freedom and self-determination. If man is not free, he will be unable to take the necessary responsibility for his actions.

In the context of the scientific-technological revolution, the function of leisure time is related to physical and cultural needs of each individual; it promotes an increase in productivity at work, easier and more rapid assimilation into new professions, and full participation in the life of the Soviet society. The current Soviet official interest in leisure time and non-working time is a by-product of the concern with the younger generation. In examining the expenditure of free time by Soviet citizens, one can find valuable information in the time allotment studies designed to obtain a detailed picture of how selected groups of citizens spend their time - which at the same time, develops and improves the personality structure. The activities belonging to leisure time may be divided into several groups: 1. Study and self-education; 2. Attending public performances; 3. Reading books; 4. Listening to radio and watching TV; 5. Tourism; 6. Sports; 7. Social gatherings; 8. Personal desires; 9. Emotional involvements, and 10. Passive rest.

From the data analyzed in Tables III. through VIII., one can conclude that the leisure time structure of workers, professionals, engineers, educated and non-educated Soviet citizens, significantly influences and forms individual personality characteristics and human values. A cross analysis of leisure time and non-working time schedules provides a personality model which is oriented toward industrial and economic change. The leisure time structure of Soviet people shows a productive tendency while they maintain their private and personal aspirations, desires, personal beliefs and value concepts.

The contemporary development of Soviet labor relations is illustrated as it pertains to the personality formation of workers and the type of work performed, the educational background related to professional performance, the conditions of work and the planning of work, as well as positive and negative personality qualities of workers.

Subsequently, positive and negative personality qualities of workers have been categorized and include such personality characteristics as initiative, discipline, intelligence, consciousness, sincerity, constructive criticism and professional performance, a critical attitude toward co-workers, organization of labor, independence at work, lack of self-control, lack of concentration, impatience, laziness, hot-temperedness, flexibility in adopting contemporary methods of management, and influence in accomplishing the work norms of the production process of enterprises.

The influence of scientific-technological accomplishments upon the biological and psychological nature of man indicates a change of human existence. The process of change was initiated by the development of computers and the competition of the two world systems; different perceptions of human existence are realized, and different influences characterize the social structure of the contemporary personality. By applying the cybernetic system within society, man changes his character, as well as his responsibility.

The scientific-technological progress is therefore the essence of the personality formation and a creative power within the contemporary Soviet society. The development of the personality structure is a basic problem of the scientific technological revolution. The link between man and machine is characterized by moral personality qualities and by a psychological reliability of the personality. The effectiveness of automation is determined not by the level of knowledge of man, but by the degree of personal responsibility, the degree of consciousness and personal initiative and the mental condition of workers who operate the control panel (automated management system).

The collective aspect and the individual aspect of the personality exist in a dialectical antithesis; they form a relationship of mutual elimination and mutual interrelation. The interrelationship of various structural models of human relations within the collective form a unified whole which can be described as a collective-individual personality structure. The social development and the reorganization of the Soviet society strive to increase the output of the national economy and allow workers to develop individual initiatives and independent decision-making within the social processes of collectives. Such initiatives are directed towards the implementation of the scientific-technological revolution and towards establishing a flexible and politically independent management system of production enterprises and collectives.

Human values of the collective personality are characterized by adherence to the political cause and the sincerity of relationships among members of the collective. The psychology of the collective has ' we ' as its starting point and not ' I '.

The managers and leaders of the Soviet technical elite must have the following professional qualifications and personality characteristics as required by official Party guidelines: 1. Ideological priorities of the leadership cadres; 2. Participation in seminars on management techniques and on the art of leadership; 3. The specialist manager should be educated in economic matters, in contemporary methods of calculation and in all aspects of cybernetics.

The leadership is a process of inner-psychological organization and the management of collectives. The leadership requires harmony between activities and behavior of people in improving social norms and applying moral principles within society. A management type of personality structure is characterized by the ability to organize labor relations which are based on scientific knowledge and advanced technological systems. The leader or manager must possess strong volitional qualities, which should be used in connection with ' power '. The leader should not only admire and respect his own personality, but also the personality of all members of the collective. The leadership qualities of managers of production enterprises are divided into two aspects: Production-related technological activities; 2. Social-psychological activities.

The structure of social-psychological functions of leadership activities is divided into four groups: 1. Informational, 2. Organizational, 3. Socializational, 4. Decision-making function.

Two general types of leadership personalities of managers of collectives are analyzed by Soviet sociologists. 1. A candidate should be selected to leadership positions because of objective personality characteristics, which means, people who will guarantee equal chances for all. 2. Those, who share the advantages of the production process with the workers of collectives.

Active participation of the Soviet delegates, based on personal innovation and initiative, can serve as an educative tool and influence the mass character of the whole society. The Soviet delegate does not issue party directives; he is supposed to teach the masses and to learn from the masses. The Soviet delegate must have the following qualifications: he must be respectful, authoritative, a good organizer; he should possess warm human qualities, realistic life experience, the basic knowledge of human psychology, and he must be able to approach each individual as an individual. The personality qualities and human culture are obtainable only by direct contact with the electorate and through the exchange of political and social views.

Soviet education is a powerful factor in personality development. A Soviet educator must possess professional qualifications which are shown by his teaching abilities, and in his logical interpretation of texts, the ability to analyze, the ability to make independent conclusions, the ability to solve problems and the ability to conduct basic research. Additional personality qualities of Soviet educators, as described by their students, are: Authority in the scientific field, sensitivity for people, persistence, knowledge of psychology, spiritual leader of young people.

Specific personality characteristics of Soviet engineers are connected with creative abilities. The intellect of engineers includes, in addition to the general erudition, logical thinking capabilities. The practical intellect is interrelated with the verbal intellect, which means that the level of practical professional knowledge and creative activities depend on the general erudition of the personality of engineers.

The inter-human relation and personality qualities of leaders of scientific institutions should be able to equalize their professional standards with their social obligation. The aspiration of leadership and authority among technical personnel and engineers appears as a personality characteristic of individuals, who are capable of solving complicated technical problems, which require a highly developed sense of responsibility. Additional personality characteristics of engineers include: integrity, adherence to principles, intelligence, politeness, technical competence, personal culture, organizational ability, initiative, psychological ability to understand people, and resourcefulness.

D THE CHINESE COMMUNIST PERSONALITY

1. THE CONFUCIAN PERSONALITY

China, once one of the most conservative nations in history, has become the most radical: determined to eliminate traditional values in institutions, social, and moral norms. Communist Chinese society under Mao Tse-tung has tried to replace the traditional Confucian type of personality with the Communist type of collective personality and mass-mentality characteristics.

The traditional Chinese personality is characterized by moderation; this means an absence of harshness, vehemence, or violence. Moderation in traditional China is a way of action that avoids going to extremes, or a state of mind in which human reasoning and feeling reach a perfect harmony of calmness and soberness. The quality of moderation in the traditional Chinese people is the product of faithfulness and sympathy - of what may be described as true and unselfish love and peacefulness of mind, leading to the positive efforts for the good of others.

The Chinese have this love because they live a life of heart, a life of feeling: feeling in the sense of human affection that prings spontaneously from the deepest part of the heart.

" Such beliefs and ideals, reiterated in each generation, constitute a set of ultimate values which were absorbed by the literary heritage of the past. Ultimate values imply a set of operating principles and a set of desirable behavior patterns which will serve the ideal order and give the individual a sure sense of contributing to its realization. For the purpose of education and socialization, a nation's ideals are translated into a set of approved attitudes and behavior patterns. This in turn affects the choices an individual makes, the roles he assumes or rejects, and the configurations of his career and his personality. "(1) Confucianism's operating principles are distilled from the whole body of the Classics or from didactic writings meant for day-to-day guidance in the conduct of life. From ANALECTS, a list of attitudes and behavior patterns can be extracted, since it contains the cornerstone of Confucian education. (Table XXVIII.)

Table XXVIII.

CONFUCIAN BEHAVIOR PATTERNS*

1. Submissiveness to authority-parents, elders, and superiors
2. Submissiveness to the mores and the norms
3. Reverence for the past and respect for history
4. Love of traditional learning
5. Esteem for the force of example
6. Primacy of broad moral cultivation over specialized comtence
7. Preference for nonviolent moral reform in state and society
8. Prudence, caution, preference for a middle course
9. Noncompetitiveness
10. Courage and sense of responsibility for a great tradition
11. Self-respect
12. Exclusiveness and fastidiousness on moral and cultural grounds
13. Punctiliousness in treatment of others

---

* Confucian Personalities. Ed., A.F. Wright, D. Twitchett, Stanford University Press, Stanford, 1962, p. 8.

Some of these attitudes and behavior patterns occur again and again in Chinese biographies. A few of them appear decisive in shaping the lives and characters of many human beings. They are so pervasive as to constitute themes or patterns in the lives presented here and to have, perhaps, a wider relevance for understanding the force of Confucian tradition in the lives of the Chinese elite.

Living examples had equally an important part in the formation of character. Submissiveness of the young to the old, of the unlearned to the learned, reinforced the imperative to pattern oneself after an approved example. This might be a father or an uncle, but it was more often a teacher.

Confucian writing in China often describes the responsibility of the cultivated person to serve as a model for others to emulate, and praises the efficacy of virtuous models in changing the behavior of large number of people. According to ANALECTS, if the person in power leads the people with rectitude, no one will dare to act otherwise. Confucius said, " When those who are in high stations perform well all their duties to their relations, the people are aroused to virtue." The Great Learning states: " When the ruler, as a father, a son, and a brother is a model, then the people imitate him. This is what is meant by saying, ' The government of his kingdom depends on his regulation of the family.' Much of the historical scholarship for which the Chinese are famous was concerned with unearthing models from the past for the education of the people, from exalted men of the past such as Kuan Yu (model of loyalty) and Shun (model of filial piety), to more local fugures."(2)

The ideal person embodies certain traits that can more properly be described as belonging to individuals. Selflessness is one of these. The selfless person submerges his own immediate interests or wishes to those of a larger unit of which he is a part. It is an old value in China, closely associated with the mystical currents of Taoism, Confucianism, and Buddhism that proclaim the essential unity of individuals by virtue of their possession of some universal attribute, such as Tao, the Buddha nature, or Principle. In its Confucian form, it derives from the moral intuition that fulfillment of one's role in a social system takes precedence over all other ethical considerations.

The existence of model persons was always important to educated Chinese. The nature and the function of sages are central in Confucian ethics. They embody all the traits of the ideal man, such as filial piety, loyalty to prince, reverence for elders, benevolence, and sincerity. The May Fourth Movement violently attacked many of the sagely virtues, such as filial piety and loyalty, as ways of keeping China hopelessly backward in the clutches of an older order. The May Fourth Movement was successful in discrediting the sage. We can view the new man, as idealized by Mao, as an attempt to fill the void by creating a replacement exemplar.

R E F E R E N C E S

1. Confucian Personalities. Ed., A.F. Wright, D. Twitchett. Stanford University Press, Stanford. 1962, p. 7.

2. W.T. de Bary, Individualism and Humanitarianism in Late Ming Thought. In: Self and Society in Ming Thought. New York, Columbia University Press, 1970.

2. THE CHINESE COMMUNIST PERSONALITY UNDER MAO TSE-TUNG

The proletarian revolution in China was to become the impetus for pushing history into Communism, the final stage, in which all class distinctions would disappear. The assumption was that man had adopted and included an entirely new value system devoid of the need or desire to acquire private property. Common property owned jointly by all the people would assure the equal and just distribution of the goods and services produced by the society. When the legal, political, and cultural institutions were the product of a new man, then these institutions would reflect new orientations and new infra-human relations.

In a directive of the Central Committee published in June 1943, the party set the guidelines for implementing the mass-line policy. The following excerpt represents the classic statement of Mao's conception of the methodology with which to link the Marxist theory of knowledge to the party's political, economic, educational and military self-sufficiency movements. " In all practical work of our Party, correct leadership can only be developed on the principle of " from the masses, to the masses." This means summing up (i.e. coordinating and systematizing after careful study) the views of the masses, then taking the resulting ideas back to the masses, explaining and popularizing them until the masses embrace the ideas as their own, stand up for them and translate them into action by way of testing their correctness. Then it is necessary once more to sum up the views of the masses, and once again take the resulting ideas back to the masses so that the masses give them their wholehearted support... And so on, over and over again, so that each time these ideas emerge with greater correctness and become more vital and meaningful. This is what the Marxist theory of knowledge teaches us." (1)

John Wilson Lewis has summed up Mao's conception of the mass line by noting that the concept is made up of four progressive stages: perception, summarization, authorization, and implementation. " (2)

The mass line concept was a methodology intended to provide both the party's cadres and the masses with a new vision of man in the future. For both the cadres and the masses, the rectification program meant the creation of a new vision of life by a new kind of person based on a working consensus and a shared value system in which everyone played a key role.

The rectification movement allowed the party to translate its wartime guerilla policies into concrete policies culminating in the mass line. Because of mass-line politics, the party was able to construct a new concept of the ideal Communist man: one who worked unselfishly for the good of all people without regard for ego. The rectification movement decisively made Mao's conception of the relationship between Marxism-Leninism and the Chinese situation the basis on which to develop the Chinese revolution. While Mao's power over the party was to be sporadically challenged after the rectification program, he had by now consolidated his position to the extent that by 1945 the REFORM DOCUMENTS had "... become Party dogma and the reform process had become a continuing organizational mechanism."(3)

Mao's formulation of contemporary personality theory is contained in his often quoted thesis that, " It is only through repeated education by positive and negative examples and through comparisons and contrasts that revolutionary parties and revolutionary people can temper themselves, become mature and make sure of victory."(4) References to the utility of establishing models are frequent enough in Mao's writings to suggest the presence of assumptions about the best way to motivate people.

Mao Tse-tung's speeches emphasized the rectification movement, which means that the whole Party should study Marxism through criticism and self-analysis. (Speech at the Chinese Communist National Party's Conference on Propaganda Work, March 17, 1957, and his speech On the Correct Handling of Contradictions Among the People, February 27, 1957.)

The remoulding campaign of intellectuals (educators and scientists) includes the integration of intellectuals with the masses of workers and peasants. However, ideological manipulation and remoulding is a long-term process, since it involves the change of the world outlook of intellectuals.
" Persuasion, not coercion, is the only way to convince. Coercion will never result in convincing people. To try to make them submit by force simply won't do. This kind of method is not permissible in dealing with comrades or friends." (5)

The policy of letting a hundred flowers blossom and a hundred schools of thought contend, offerend additional guarantees for change from the traditional Chinese human value system and personality characteristics to Communist ideological principles and guidelines within the arts and sciences.

Mao Tse-tung attached great importance also to literature as a political tool. He judged the work of authors mainly in terms of their social-political usefulness and tried to create a literature which would fulfill a utilitarian function for the development of the Chinese Communist society.

A precondition of personality transformation is the readiness of the human mind for self-evaluation. The practice of self-analysis becomes habitual through the imitation of models. Chinese writings convey a belief that people tend to evaluate by thinking in terms of comparisons between two poles.
" Comparison with one pole in a set of polarities is an element in evaluation. Those who concentrate on models will learn to see the imbalances between their own virtues or work capacity and those of the models (in both quality and quantity). Mao described the awareness of this disequilibrium between the model and the emulator in dialectical terms, pointing out the subsequent redress, that in turn followed by a new disequilibrium."(6)

However, there is a major obstacle in achieving the transformation process of the Chinese traditional mentality concept into the mass-mentality value orientation of contemporary Chinese Communist man. The basic value change within the transformation process is seen by Mao Tse-tung as eliminating all personal and subjective features of the traditional Confucian personality into a mass-oriented group personality and mentality. " According to dialectical materialism, thought must reflect objective reality and must be tested and verified in objective practice before it can be taken as truth, otherwise it cannot. Though we have done well in the last few years, subjectivism is evident everywhere. There will be subjectivism in the future, just as there is today. Subjectivism will always be there, ten thousand years and even a hundred million years from now, and it will be so long as humanity does not perish. Where there is subjectivism, there are mistakes."(7)

With this statement, Mao Tse-tung predicted the failure of his revolutionary mass-line campaign in changing and remoulding the character and the personality of Chinese people. Mao understood the historical destiny in not being able to change or transform the nature of man, that is, to eliminate all egoistic desires from individual human beings and to reshape their way of thinking and behaving. Mao concluded, therefore, that by failing to eliminate such negative elements from the masses, especially from the personality of man, man cannot be completely altered or remoulded.

Mao's negation of basic human qualities led him not only to the usual insistence of men's differing class nature, but also to the decidedly unusual attention to differences among individuals within classes. In one of the earliest official analyses of human nature by a leading Party theoretician, Ch'en Po-ta directed attention to personality variations within classes: " Each and every individual's personality in a class society has a definite class nature, because in a class society everyone belongs to a definite class, and all go through life under definite historical conditions. The unity of class nature and personality is one side of the matter. On the other side, in various kinds of societies there is a variety of different conditions, different phenomena, different kinds of work for the people, different kinds of lives, and different kinds of struggles; and the concrete environments, large or small, to which each person belongs

(social, natural), the concrete angels of life with which each comes in contact, all have various and different social features. This will influence each person's personality in every sort of society. Some will have abilities leaning in one way, others in other ways; and, with regard to each person's character, some are brave and some are weak, some are deceitful and some are upright...etc. In sum, the many sorts of social life determine the many types of human personalities."(8)

However, when the Maoists speak of the changeability of man they often refer to changes that may take place during a short period of time in individuals; they are not necessarily referring to long-term changes in the natures of the species or of social groups. The notion of thought that is introduced into discussions of the social nature and personality transformation also reinforces the place of the particular in the Chinese concept of man.

Mao Tse-tung named five requirements for successors to the Chinese revolutionary cause. Revolutionaries must wholeheartedly serve the majority of the people of China and the whole world; they must be proletarian statesmen capable of uniting and working together with the majority; they must be models in applying the Party's democratic centralism and leadership based on the mass line; and they must be modest and prudent and have the courage to correct mistakes. People with such qualifications are the new type of man that Chinese education must produce. The Peking Review (February 18, 1966) editorialized: " As the pace of socialist revolution and social construction in China grows swifter, a new type of man is emerging in growing numbers. They are highly political minded, dedicated heart and soul to the revolution, and they perform remarkable feasts despite great odds."

What are the specific characteristics that education must strive to cultivate in the new man? Besides such general concepts as " good pupils of the age of Mao Tse-tung " or " good daughters of the Communist Party," several formulations of specific characteristics have been publicized at different times. Before the Cultural Revolution, much was said about " five-good youth ": one who was obedient to the Party, a dilligent worker, able to overcome difficulties, alert in protection of public property, and mindful of the unity of the Youth League. During the Cultural Revolution, the " four-good " became the goal of education: youth was to be trained to be good in ideological work, good in military training, good in arranging everyday life, and good in working style.

" The supreme virtue of the new man is wholehearted dedication to the revolution led by Chairman Mao and the Chinese Communist Party. This dedication means absolute loyalty and obedience to the Chairman and the Party. From Liu Shao-ch'i to Lin Piao and down to the present time, a good revolutionary is always expected to put away all personal plans and ambitions and to put the interest of the revolution and the Party above all. The Cultural Revolution called for the criticism of revisionism and the struggle against selfishness."(9) The new Chinese man is undaunted by difficulties, undeterred by hardship or personal danger. Indeed, death for the sake of the revolution must be considered a great honor. Most of the heroes and models selected for public emulation were honored posthumously for their readiness to make the supreme sacrifice.

The new Chinese man seeks no personal fame or glory. In the words of an industrial hero, " I'm willing to be an ' ox ' serving the people all my life." He was described as an indefatigable worker " nurtured by Mao Tse-tung Thought," one who displayed the " revolutionary spirit of fearing neither hardship nor death" and gave all his life for the revolutionary cause.

The Chinese ideological transformation and the formation process of the new human value system under communist leadership was under strict Stalinist guidance in the early period of the People's Republic of China. The various educational reforms, the literary and intellectual re-orientations have used Soviet patterns as models for their value change. However, there is a tendency of change today with regard to Soviet and Chinese value concepts, in connection with the industrialization of both societies, in connection with social dynamics and ideological differences, especially after the official break of the two Communist Parties.

R E F E R E N C E S

1. Mao Tse-tung, On Methods of Leadership. Selected Works, IV, p. 113.
2. J.W. Lewis, Leadership in Communist China. Ithaca, Cornell University Press, 1963, p. 72.
3. Boyd Compton, Mao's China: Party Reform Documents, 1942-1944. University of Washington Press, Seattle, 1966, pp. 13-14.
4. Chi Ping, Attach Importance to the Role of Teachers by Negative Example. Peking Review, No. 13. (March 31, 1972), p. 5.
5. Mao Tse-tung, Speech at Party National Conference on Propaganda Work. March 12, 1957, In: Selected Works of Mao Tse-tung, Volume V. p. 433. Foreign Language Press, Peking, 1977.
6. D.J. Munro, The Concept of Man in Contemporary China. The University of Michigan Press, Ann Arbor, 1977, p. 139.
7. Mao Tse-tung, Strengthen Party Unity and Carry Forward Party Traditions. August 30, 1956, Selected Works of Mao Tse-tung, Volume 5, p. 316. Foreign Language Press, Peking, 1977.
8. Ch'en Po-ta, Human nature, party nature, individual nature. Hong Kong: Ch'ao-hsi she, 1947, p. 5.
9. Theodore Hsi-en Chen, The Maoist Educational Revolution. Praeger Publishers, New York, p. 74.

a. Chinese Communist Society and Personality Development

A new Chinese society presupposes new men with new minds, new ideas, new emotions, and new attitudes. The making and remaking of new men therefore becomes a fundamental task of the Communist revolution and the central aim of education.

Below are listed seven personality characteristics of the new Chinese Communist man, which should be accomplished by means of life experience within the communist society.

1. " Absolute selflessness. The new man has no ambitions beyond that of serving the revolution.
2. Obedience to the Communist Party. Obedience to the leadership is an indispensable characteristic of good citizenship. Loyalty to the revolution and loyalty to the Communist Party is one and the same thing.
3. Class consciousness. The Chinese Communists equate political consciousness with class consciousness. A person of high political consciousness is keenly aware of class distinctions and ready to engage in the class struggle.
4. Ideological study. The new man must be guided by the correct ideological outlook, which depends on unceasing study. The Constitution of the Chinese Communist Party stipulates that the first duty of party members is " to study Marxism-Leninism and unceasingly raise the level of their understanding."
5. Labor and production. The Chinese Communist exalt labor both for its ideological value and for its contribution to production. Labor is believed to have therapeutic value in ideological remoulding. The proletarian society expects all people to engage in labor.
6. Versatility. The ideal man is a person able to serve in varied capacities. He can be shifted from one productive activity to another in response to the changing needs of the party-state.
7. Red expert. The socialist man must be both Red and expert. Expertness refers to the specific knowledge and skills that enable the person to make positive contributions to production and socialist construction."(1)

Within the process of socialization of the Chinese society, we can observe that associated with the need to control human emotions and communist values is the equally central factor that in the Chinese personality there is little room for ambiguity. Since every relationship has its correct form, the total system of relationships must fit together to form a perfect design. As long as one acts to the rules of proper conduct, everything should be clear-cut and well defined. " Since the prime restraint in the Chinese socialization process is to ensure that there will be no spontaneous expression of any form of emotion, it is dangerous, and most unmanly, to allow emotions to determine behavior. Man is supposed to be able to calculate in detail what act is rationally and ritualistically appropriate to the situation." (2) Political socialization in China is directed at gaining the total commitment of the population to Mao's vision. Mao's vision is that under the leadership of the Chinese Communist Party, China should become a totally selfless society in which all individual, group, and factional interests are absent. There is more than just a hint of Confucian virtue in this goal, and in this sense Mao may be seen as culture-centric. " The Chinese Communist morality demands that the individual approach his work with a new socialist work attitude, striving for a high rate of production. This new attitude toward labor is to replace such erroneous views as that of labor being a difficult burden that is to be feared, so that labor is a glorious, honorable, and courageous activity, which should be seen as everyone's right and obligation. The individual should take part in labor, because it is the basis of the socialist cause."(3)

To evaluate whether a person's behavior towards society and towards other people conforms to the principles of communist motality, it must be determined whether such behavior, in all aspects, conforms to the interests of creating and fulfilling the great causes of socialism and communism. All behavior that conforms to the interests of this revolutionary struggle conforms to the principles of communist morality.

The personality characteristics which conform to the interest of the revolutionary struggle of the new Chinese mass man are listed below (Table XXIX).

Table XXIX.

PERSONALITY CHARACTERISTICS OF CHINESE REVOLUTIONARIES *

1. Industrious in work and study
2. Diligent and persistent
3. Achievement and goal oriented

4. Dedicated to building the new society
5. Cooperative in work with others for common goals
6. Honest and responsible in personal affairs, in relations with others
7. Has a sense of responsibility
8. Willing to accept the advice and criticism of others
9. Prudent and forsighted
10. Patient and not hot-tempered
11. Obedient, deferring to rules and to elders and superiors
12. Thrifty and frugal
13. Courageous, willing to sacrifice his life for others
14. Altruistic, being kind to others, particular the aged and less fortunate
15. Expresses anger or behaves aggressively only toward those who violate communist social standards or who attempt to harm the society
16. Vigilant towards enemy attack and deception
17. Ingenious in solving problems
18. Sees happines and personal satisfaction as sufficient recompense for sacrifice or accomplishment.

---

* Charles Ridley, Paul H.B. Godwin, Debbis J. Doolin, The Making of a Model Citizen in Communist China. Hoover Institution Press, Stanford, 1971, p. 192.

To summarize the above list of character traits and personality values of the Chinese communist mass-political man and revolutionary, we see a deep concern for the industrial development of China, personal initiative, competitiveness, emotional stability, and a love which is to serve as the basic motive in the complete subordination of the individual to the state.

Additional personality qualities essential to the attainment of national goals are: firmness, courage, humility, sincerity, frugality and simplicity. These personality characteristics have been borrowed from the Confucian concept of human values.

The cultivation of these moral personality qualities is for

the guidance of young people in their daily lives. It further stresses the importance of cultivating in young people a love for obedience to regulations and laws. However, these virtues are conceived of not as superficial adornments of the personality, but rather as a matter of policies; these values are the bedrock upon which all other values are based. Schurman rightly stresses that values and norms of the "... total ideology are tools which motivate individuals to commitment and are given rational ideas for action. Values of the ideology are designed to bring about a moral and psychological transformation of the individual. By acquiring a pure ideology and internalizing its values, the individual develops commitment to the organization." (4)

A key to understanding the important role of re-education in Communist China is the Chinese Marxists' dictum that ' thought determines action '. The editorial of the official paper Jen Min Jih Pao (People's Daily) is typical of this reasoning: " Work is done by man, and man's action is governed by his thinking. A man without the correct political thinking is a man without a soul. In every work we undertake, we must always insist that politics take command and let political work come before anything else. The emphasis is on the experience of the masses, demonstrative examples and living personalities in the Party's attempt to elevate the level of consciousness of the masses as an important bearing on the policy and pattern of Communist mass persuasion."(5)

Man's social consciousness is determined by social existence. Because of their participation in the practice of labor and their close contact with the workers and peasants, " people first experience a great change in the spiritual aspect and are taught the class viewpoint of the working class, the labor viewpoint, the mass viewpoint, the collective viewpoint, and the dialectical materialist viewpoint."(6) In Communist China mass campaigns are also an expression of a basic attitude toward national development, an attitude which emphasizes mass and emotional participation regardless of the professional specialization of individuals or the different natures of various tasks. " Setting the masses in motion represents the beginning of a collective process of implanting in the public mind new motivation for group behavior and that constitutes a cornerstone of the Communist mass propaganda technique."(7)

However, if we were to characterize the outcome of the Chinese Cultural Revolution in terms of some concept of an ideal man which it aimed at producing, then we would be forced to conclude that its achievements have been limited. China has not become a country where all has been abandoned to the tenets of Marxism-Leninism-Mao Tse-tung thought. " It would be unrealistic to assume that one short campaign could achieve that ideal or, indeed, that the ideal man could really exist. There has not been a great qualitative change but a re-assessment of developments which were already taking place."(8)

REFERENCES

1. Theodore Hsi-en Chen, The New Socialist Man. In: Gerry K. Bertsch, Comparative Communism, The Soviet, Chinese and Yugoslav Models. Freeman and Company, San Francisco, 1976, pp. 300-301.
2. Lucian W. Pye, The Spirit of Chinese Politics. A Psychocultural Study of the Authority Crisis in Political Development, The MIT Press, Cambridge, 1968, p. 96.
3. Charles Price Ridley, Paul H.B. Godwin, Debbis J. Doolin, The Making of a Model Citizen in Communist China. Hoover Institution Press, Stanford, 1971, p. 56.
4. Franz Schurman, Ideology and Organization in Communist China. University of California Press, Berkeley, 1971, p. 45.
5. Frederick T.C. TU, Mass Persuasion in Communist China. Praeger, New York, 1964, p. 4.
6. Steward Fraser, Ed., Chinese Communist Education. Vanderbilt University Press, Nashville, 1965, p. 331.
7. C.K. Yang, Chinese Communist Society: The Family and the Village. MIT-Press, p. 204.
8. S.R. Schram, Ed., Authority Participation and Cultural Change in China. Cambridge University Press, 1975, p. 329.

3. CHINESE LITERARY DOCTRINE AND COMMUNIST VALUES

In 1942, the basic principles of Chinese Communist literary doctrine were already laid down in Mao's Yenan Talks. At that point, Mao's literary mentor was Lenin, whose theories he accepted together with their Stalinist-Zhdanovian exegesis. In his Yenan Talks, Mao projected the furtherance of the revolution as the aim of literature. He explained the necessity for political demands to prevail over artistic ones; he stressed the value of folklore, and he justified his rejection of the criticism of the evil aspects of the revolution and of communist rule by referring to the Soviet example. Mao also cited the principles of socialist realism, party spirit, and typicality - the three essential constituents of Soviet literary theory. It was in the Yenan Talks that the main theses of Chinese literary doctrine were codified.

The principle of party spirit permeates the entire Chinese literary doctrine to such an extent that its basic theses are largely political. This becomes apparent in Ch'ien Chun-jui's summary of methods of creating socialist literature and art. He lists the following ten ptinciples:

1. " Literature and art should serve the workers, peasants, soldiers, and other working people.
2. Literature and art should serve socialism.
3. Literature and art should combine popularization and elevation.
4. It should unite ideological nature and artistry - the political criteria first and the artistic criteria second.
5. It should integrate the literary and artistic workers with the masses of the workers and peasants.
6. It should permit the hundred flowers blossom and the hundred schools of thought contend.
7. It should combine the critical inheritance of the legacy and original creation.
8. It should combine revolutionary romanticism and revolutionary realism.
9. It should let politics assume command.

10. It should follow the mass line." (1)

None of these principles is exclusively concerned with artistic matters. In advising the integration or combination of what seem to be incompatible or hardly reconcilable entities, vagueness and ambiguity prevail. Yet, the principles listed under number three, four, and seven, which were maintained throughout the 1956-1960 period and can even be found in Mao's Yenan Talks, call for some remarks about the role of language in the literary doctrine and about the function of literature. The principle that popularization (the use of simple language and assimilation of folk traditions) should be combined with elevation (raising the cultural level of the readers) is, in effect, acting as a brake upon elevation since Mao, in 1942, stated that popularization should prevail over elevation.

Within Chinese literary doctrine we distinguish between artistic and political notions, and it should not be taken for granted that, after putting aside the obvious political concepts, the remainder is all aesthetic theory describing the attributes of literary works. In keeping with Mao's professed utilitarianism, what remains after political concepts are sifted out is largely theory on how the attributes of literary phenomena can most effectively be employed to further the revolution. " The Chinese communist theory of literature treats literature hardly as it is, but rather as it should be, that is, less as an isolated phenomenon than in its sociological function of promoting communism. The Chinese literary doctrine is prescriptive rather than descriptive." (2)

Hence, literature cannot be considered as being autonomous, and all endeavors of Chinese writers to view it as such and to free it from party control were bound to meet vehement criticism. According to Chinese Marxism, artistic creation cannot be justified by its own traditional place in the human world, since human life is not the standard for all things, but it is itself subject to a theoretical higher ideal. Thus it maintains the reverse of Pasternak's dictum that, " man is born to live, not to prepare for life..."(3) For life, as Chou Yang has put it, is too dangerous as the high seas and threatens to engulf communist man. Only with Marxism as the compass and the Communist Party as the pilot can writers be saved from losing their direction.

China's literary doctrine tends to gloss over immediate needs and overlooks such basic experiences as the yearning for love and the fear of death. Lyrical expression of love, as such, is considered intolerable. The satirical essay which castigates social evils is severely limited in its range of subject matter and style. The hero of the story must embody a positive message, for everything is supposed to be brightened by the sun of approaching communism.

The hero in Communist Chinese literature exemplifies the new political culture and symbolizes the modern world outlook. The hero in Communist Chinese literature is primarily a pedagogical tool for political education. The Party uses it mainly to teach people the values which are necessary for national development. The heroes eagerly learn the Party's doctrine and policies, carry out such policies with enthusiasm, do their utmost to activate the masses and to arouse their political understanding. " The Chinese literary heroes are serious-minded, practical, innovative and progressive. They have a great eagerness to learn new things and new technology."(4)

In Chinese Communist literature, the heroes are depicted as essentially ordinary men and women. With regard to moral qualities of heroes, the writers particularly emphasize the four major personality characteristics: courage, dedication, activism, and discipline. On a larger scale, the arts can serve as the drummer of the age:" Revolutionary literature and art must help people make new history. Such is the grand role of the arts in relation to their era. The role, not only of a barometer showing incipient changes and those already in progress, but also a lever in helping to produce change."(5)

The Chinese contemporary human value concept and the new communist personality were partly formed by artistic creativity and the political doctrine imposed on the arts. Mao Tse-tung presented the definition of the politization process of literature as follows: " Ideological expressions in the form of artistic creativity or literary work are the product of the human brain reflecting the life of a given society. Revolutionary art and literature are the products of the brains of revolutionary artists and writers reflecting the life of the people."(6)

Raymond J. Lammers related the transformation process of the Chinese mentality to literary fiction. " The persuasive purpose of each play involves issues that are politically important to the Chinese leaders. These issues pertain to women's rights, the suppression of counter-revolutionaries, the eradication of bureaucratic corruption, the discrediting of traditional values, the development of a political consciousness among the Chinese intellectuals and the demand that the Chinese put aside their individuality in favor of a communistic collectivism."(7) The idea that the Chinese can improve their conditions through an uncompromising dedication to the collective will of the Communists is clearly evident in Chu Yuan's Steeled in Battles, The Test, The Women's Representative, Saturday Afternoon at the Mill, The Bright Skies.

All plays in which there is a struggle between the " new " and " old " may be considered to contribute to this campaign. This is the intellectual remoulding as applied to all Chinese people. Propaganda and propaganda plays are persuasive efforts in Chinese Communist literature. Persuasion is defined by Brembeck and Howell as " the conscious attempt to modify thought and action through the manipulation of the motives of men toward determined ends." The authorities assert that man acts as the result of appeals directed toward a set of " socially-determined " motives that not only serve to take care of his physical wants but also help develop a social selfhood.

R E F E R E N C E S

1. Ch'ien Chun-ju, Wen-i pao, 1960, 8, p.4.
2. Douwe Wessel Fokkema, Literary Doctrine in China and Soviet Influence, 1956-1960. Mouton & Co., The Hague, 1965, p. 264.
3. Boris Pasternak, Doctor Zhivago. New York, Pantheon, 1958, p. 297.
4. A. Ya-li LU, Political Control of Literature in Communist China, 1949-1966. Ph.D. Thesis, Indiana University, 1972, p. 312.
5. Jack Gray, Patrick Cavendish, Chinese Communism in Crisis. Praeger, New York, p. 74.

6. Mao Tse-tung, Talks at the Yenan Forum on Art and Literature. Foreign Language Press, Peking, 1960, p. 21.

7. Raymond J. Lammers, An Analysis of a Representative Sample of Plays Written and Used for Propagandistic Purposes by the Chinese Communists. University of Minnesota, Ph.D. Thesis, 1962.

4. CHINESE EDUCATIONAL PSYCHOLOGY AND PERSONALITY DEVELOPMENT

The Central Committee of the Chinese Communist Party issued various guidelines and directives on educational policy within the People's Republic of China. The Party line for education reads as follows: " The Party line in educational policy seeks to make education serve the proletariat politically, and to unite education with productive labor. In order to implement this policy, education must be lead by the Party. Marxist-Leninist political and ideological indoctrination must be carried out in all schools to indoctrinate the teachers and students with the class viewpoint of workers, the mass viewpoint, the collectivist viewpoint, the labor viewpoint or the viewpoint calling for the integration of mental labor with physical labor, and the dialectic materialistic viewpoint. The future direction is for schools to run factories and farms, and for factories and agricultural co-operatives to establish schools."(1)

The Chinese Communist teacher has to play many parts in his career - political mentor, educator, substitute parent, family counselor, arbiter of grades, job placement advisor, and moulder of revolutionaries. These responsibilities, plus managing the delicate relationship among Party, student, and self, generate strong internal and external pressures; but above all is the pressure to confer, compromise and conform. China's famous and most influential teacher, Confucius, imparted a principle which has to shape the Chinese attitude toward teaching and learning for centuries to come: " I have transmitted what was taught to me without making up anything of my own. I have been faithful to and loved the Ancients."(2)

Some Chinese scholars have blamed the inherent conservatism in Confucianism - the transmittal of an all-embracing set of values and rules of behavior as good for all time - for locking out new ideas and new patterns of actions and for blocking China's modernization for so long.

China's socialist education is designed to foster workers with socialist consciousness and culture. In such education, moral education is of primary importance. P'an Shu elaborated basic directions of the Chinese moral education and personality values of revolutionary men and women in his speech " Some Suggestions Concerning the Unfolding of Research Work in Educational Psychology. " (delivered at a meeting of educational psychologists convened by the Chinese Psychological Society).

" We must gradually train the younger generation to acquire the virtue of loving the socialist motherland, loving the laboring people, loving the Communist Party, loving the leaders, loving labor, loving science, and taking good care of public property, to acquire the patriotic and internationalist spirit, to support the leadership of the Party, to serve socialism and the people with willingness, and to establish gradually communist morality, the viewpoint of the working class, the mass viewpoint, the labor viewpoint and the dialectical materialistic viewpoint. It is necessary for educational psychology to analyze the students' psychological structure of morality, and to study the psychological laws governing the students' grip on moral ideas and the formation of their moral belief, moral sense, and moral behavior and habits, as well as the interrelations between them. It is necessary to study the process of development of the will of the students and of the formation of the communist style. It is necessary to study the collective role of students in the process of forming their moral qualities, the psychological feature of self-conscious discipline and its process of formation. We have carried out very little research in these aspects. In the past few years, we carried out a small amount of investigation and research of a general nature and experimental research of an exploratory nature. A good job must be done in intensifying research work in this connection."(3)

During the Cultural Revolution, the Ministry of Education, the Ministry of Higher Education, and the Departments and Bureau of Education on lower levels were abolished, and revolutionary committees and " education groups " took over educational administration. Some major features of the Maoist educational program can be summarized as follows:

1. The primary aim of education is to produce an educated proletariat, not an intellectual elite.
2. Revolutionary education is action-oriented, not knowledge centered: practice-centered, not study centered.
3. It is geared to present needs, not future needs.
4. It avoids dependence on foreign models and foreign materials.
5. It puts ideology and politics in command of all school work.
6. It does not recognize intellectual development as its primary aim.
7. It places little value on academic quality and scholarship standards.
8. It repudiates the bourgeois tradition of selfish individualism.

In 1968, when the Proletarian Cultural Revolution was developing in depth, the question of how to carry forward the cadres' educational and ideological revolutionization and revolutional government institutions was discussed on a wide scale throughout China. In October of 1968 Mao Tse-tung issued the following policy direction: " Going down to do manual labor gives vast numbers of cadres an excellent opportunity to study once again: this should be done by all cadres except those who are old, weak, ill or disabled. Cadres at their posts should also go down in turn to do manual labor."

The science of psychology has had over two decades to develop and grow within the Communist Chinese society, but it is still too young to have established its own school of thought. Since its importation from the Soviet Union in the early fifties, Chinese psychology has not departed from its philosophical base of dialectical materialism or the political orthodoxy of Marxism-Leninism and has stood in firm opposition to Western psychology. The science of psychology has followed the Soviet lead in the field, although some differences in emphasis and in direction of application are visible. However, one may not conclude that psychology in the People's Republic of China has established theoretical independence from the Soviet tradition or raised a challenging voice to Soviet leadership commensurate to the challenge on the ideological front.

" Educational psychology and research on personality values and moral characteristics of Chinese people began to develop after the Great Leap Forward, when psychologists turned to research on the learning of curriculum subjects and character training. Research has been done on the nature of moral character, which had become a question of national concern in the early sixties and which was potentially a matter of greater and more direct social consequence. The main task of educational psychology at the beginning of the 1960s was to find ways to fit itself into educational reform. P'an Shu, President of the Psychological Society called the task " the work of reforming the instruction in middle and elementary schools." He said in a speech at the Educational Psychology Specialty Conference in 1962 that experimental work was " penetrating in a planned way," (4) and he listed the chief psychological problems that merited investigation:

" In moral education, priority was to be given to ' love of socialist fatherland, love of the laboring masses, love of the Communist Party, love of the leaders, and love for physical labor, science and public property.' At the same time, there was to be training for patriotism and international spirit, willingness to support the leadership of the Party and to serve socialism and the people. Educational psychology was assigned the task of analyzing the psychological structure of the moral qualities of students, laws governing their grasp of moral concepts, formation of moral sense, moral faith and conduct, development of the will and formation of Communist character, effects of the collectivity and moral qualities, and psychological characteristics of self-discipline.

Inquiries were to be made into the psychological characteristics of labor of students: How does labor promote moral qualities? How do different forms of labor influence psychological development? And how does labor education adapt itself to individual differences and age differences? - The broad problem of motivation for learning, mastering skills, and development of thinking ability were to be attacked as well as a specific problem of how to teach various curriculum subjects. A further problem was the coordination between preschool education and school education, and the phases of learning. The need to discover and develop talents in various fields, and to analyze the causes of bad behavior and poor learning. Psychological development of the child and pedagogical reform in elementary school..."(5)

The speech indicated the direction of attention and the definition of the widened field of research within educational psychology. Yu Wen-wei proposed that educational psychology should ascertain the developmental laws concerning the acquisition of Communist consciousness and moral qualities in the student, and psychological laws concerning his mastery of knowledge and techniques.

a. The Psychological Concept of the Chinese Communist Morality

"The emphasis on the active consciousness of man in Communist Chinese psychology placed moral responsibility upon the individual, as an active feature in the relationship between social reality - psychological processes - and behavioral patterns. The Communist theory of behavior, as differentiated from a mechanistic-deterministic point of view, as well as its behavioral variations were viewed and analyzed with two different variables: nonclass variables, such as sex, age, intelligence, academic achievement, developmental phases; and class variables, in the sense that class background determines either primarily or exclusively one's active consciousness, which in turn determines behavior.

During the 1950s, the term " moral education " was seldom found in Chinese psychological literature. Early attention on this general area was almost entirely in the nature of arguments for the clas standpoint and arose in connection with the debate on the nature of human consciousness. The natural science faction of psychology emphasized that all psychological studies of the consciousness must be seen through the intervention of brain processes, while the social science faction insisted that the analysis of psychological processes include the class viewpoint or concentrate on the social content of consciousness."(6)

Little work was done in that period on the moral makeup of the individual. Psychology was aimed at answering the question of whether or not children had class consciousness. Ch'en Yuan-hui declared that class analysis was not appropriate in the study of child psychology. (7) Chu Chih-hsien stated: " Children's psychological development follows racial history: first simple sensations of class consciousness, he continued, took two routes: from early age, " He hears this is mine, and that is yours, " which are manifestations of adult consciousness. In propertyless classes, children learn how to love labor, help others, and so on. After systematic education, which Chu said came after the primary grades, children begin to acquire " stable class consciousness tendencies such as needs, motives, imagination, beliefs, and world views."(8)

REFERENCES

1. The Directive of the CCP Central Committee and the State Council on Educational Work, September 19, 1958. In: Peking People's Daily, Sept. 20, 1958.
2. Confucius, The Analects. Book VII. Chapter I. Translated by A. Waley, Random House, N.Y. 1938.
3. P'an Shu, Some Suggestions Concerning the Unfolding of Research Work in Educational Psychology. Peking, Kuang-ming Jih-pao, March 13, 1962, Survey of China Mainland Press, No. 2709 (March 30, 1962), p. 1.
4. Robert Chin and Ai-li S. Chin, Psychological Research in Communist China, 1949-1966.The MIT Press, Cambridge, 1969, p. 134.
5. P'an Shu, Ideas about expanded research in educational psychology. Kuang-ming jih-pao, March 13, 1962. Joint Publications Research Service No. 13531.
6. Ibid. p. 167.
7. Ch'en Yuan-hui, Kuang-ming jih-pao, Apr. 7, 1959.
8. Chu Chih-hsien, On the Question of the class nature of human psychology. Kuang-ming jih-pao. June 23, 1959.

5. PSYCHOLOGY OF THE CHINESE PERSONALITY

Toward the end of 1950s the only known study on the psychology of the personality was that of Li Yi on psychological characteristics of the attitude structure of good workers and poor workers among fifth and sixth-grade pupils participating in agricultural work. Li observed and interviewed two groups of eight children, each of whom had been recommended by their teacher as " good workers " and " poor workers " in a work situation. The children were asked to describe what they considered characteristics of good workers and poor workers; what their own good points and bad points were while working, and what the good point and bad points of specific good worker and of specific poor worker were. Li found the distinguishing features of good workers and poor workers to be a positive attitude toward work, rest period, tools, schedules, a sense of responsibility toward production output, common property, and the results of the labor of others, a positive attitude toward rules, and a good relation to others in work. The last point was of some intrinsic interest to the psychology of the personality, a good worker not only voluntarily helped others but also made demands upon others. Li further pointed out that good and poor workers differed most in collective spirit, next in obedience toward rules, and least in individual work schedules. (1)

The point the children themselves considered to be features of good and poor workers turned out to be Li's major contribution toward a beginning in the psychology of personality characteristics. The group of good workers saw both good and bad points in the poor worker. The group of teacher-selected poor workers saw only good points in the model student and only bad points in the other. A tendency towards realistic, full-rounded appraisal of fellow students was displayed by the exemplars among the children and a tendency toward stereotyping was noted among those who did not live up to expectations. The study could have fitted into the development of systematic knowledge on perceptual and cognitive processes of the desired type of personality: critical, seeing contradictions and faults, high conscious awareness, and still a good worker.

" It was toward the end of the recovery period from the Great Leap Forward, when the class question had temporarily receded from psychological circles and doors were opened to the broad examination of character training, that truly psychological variables rather than political ones were used to study observable aspects of normative behavior, formation of moral judgement, and motivations for moral behavior."(2)

Moral education became the most important topic of research to be developed within psychology in the early 1960s. P'an Shu said in a statement to the press (3) that psychological problems in moral education have the priority of psychological investigation. With the objective of training workers with socialist consciousness and culture, the educational psychologist was to analyze the psychological structure of the moral qualities of students, laws governing their grasp of moral concepts, formation of moral sense, moral faith, and conduct, development of the will and formation of Communist character, effects of the collectivity on moral qualities, and psychological characteristics of self-discipline.

During the early years of Chinese psychology, psychologists were preoccupied with an examination of isolated psychological processes; therefore, the whole individual was left unexplored. The scientifically oriented psychologist, who concentrated on psychological processes with emphasis on functions of the brain and higher nervous system, were criticized for neglecting individuality. Individuality meant the whole individual as compared to abstract processes such as sensation, perception, memory, or problems in the nervous system. The critics, with ideological backing, insisted that psychology should study the concrete individual, with his class background and class consciousness, and should employ the class method of analysis. The crucial question at stake, at that time, was whether the individual shared universal psychological processes with his fellow man or whether a person's class background colored all his psychological processes. Psychologists with the latter view were really arguing for the necessity to study the wholeness of the individual, without meaning of course, that it was important to study the uniqueness of each individual, with all characteristics that made him different from other individuals.

The concept of Soviet man was used as a model for the Chinese concept of man in both its projection of the time period of human nature transformation and also in its introduction of consciousness as one of the leading figures of those transformation efforts within the psychology of personality. In their statements, the Chinese psychologists would agree with the claim by Soviet scholars that in attempting to control man, the object of one's effort should be his conscious thoughts: " Soviet psychology is in contradiction to bourgeois psychology in this regard - bourgeois psychology takes the ' unconscious ' as a point of departure, as though it were the central core of man's personality, but Soviet psychology... has indicated the dominant role which conscious influences play as compared with unconscious influences... Soviet pedagogy holds the principle that it is the conscious personality of man, his conscious behavior, and his conscious discipline that are to be moulded."(4)

During the period of Chinese borrowing from the Soviet Union, Chinese psychologists had difficulties in characterizing the neurological plasticity of man. One of the major works on personality at that time was How to Understand the Personality of Students, written by Chang Chih-kuang of the Psychology Department of the Peking Normal University. According to Munro, Chang Chih-kuang drew on a distinction between four basic dispositional types of people: choleric, vigorous, phlegmatic, and melancholic. The four types are based on three innate characteristics of the nervous system: a. its ability to establish a conditioned reflex when presented with a strong stimulus; b. balance/imbalance, or, on the one hand the ease with which it can be influenced by either a positive or negative stimulus, or on the other its tendency to be more excited by or more inhibited by positive or negative stimuli; c. flexibility, or the capacity to produce the same reflex to a new stimulus. Finally, four neurological types differentiated by Pavlov are associated with the four dispositional types: aggressive and unrestrained, active and effective, quietly determined, weak and timid. But once having pointed to the innate basis of dispositional types, Chang went on to affirm their plasticity. People can change types. When she talks of abilities, in order not to suggest that they are immutable, she calls them " subjective conditions ". Character can be changed under the influence of school environment, group activities, such as Youth League, outside reading, one's occupation, and the propaganda presented in radio and theater.(5)

R E F E R E N C E S

1. Li Yi, An analysis of the psychological characteristics of primary school 5-6th grade students participating in agricultural work. Hsin-li hsueh-pao, No. 5. (1959), pp.293-302.
2. Robert and Ai-li S. Chin, p. 170.
3. P'an Shu, Ideas about expanded research in educational psychology. Kuang-ming jih-pao, Mar. 13, 1962, Joint Publications Research Service No. 13531.
4. Li Shih-sheng, Transform oneself into a new man through labor. Hung ch'i (Red Flag), No. 18, 1960, p. 34.
5. Munro, p. 64.

6. PERSONALITY TRAITS OF CHINESE TECHNICAL PERSONNEL

To be able to define the value concept of technical personnel in Chinese factories and institutions, where technological personality values are being formed and needed as part of the managerial abilities, and where patterns of behavior of technical personnel are being moulded, we must direct our attention to the micro-level, intra organizational behavior, to the values guiding the behavior, and to the linkages of one institution to another (See Table XXX.) on: Competing Value Systems as they Apply to the Organization of Scientific Activities. These value systems are referred to as professional, the bureaucratic, and the ideological personality values.

These developments in China were an attempt to realize the values that pertained to science and the role of science in society found in Party doctrine. These values, and the means followed to implement them, opened up the possibility of a different approach to institutionalization. Such values are consistent with some of the professional values in being antibureaucratic, and with some of the bureaucratic values in being opposed to certain aspects of professionalism. " In early 1960's, as part of the general retrenchment following the Great Leap

Forward, serious attempts to institutionalize the ideological values were abandoned. Instead, in the effort to get the science systems to work, the type of accomodation between the professional and bureaucratic systems which would have been anticipated in 1957, but whose emergence was delayed by the promotion of ideological values, began to appear. It was precisely such an accomodation which troubled the Maoists and which led to the reassertion of ideological values during the Cultural Revolution. The long period of re-building the science system since the Cultural Revolution can be seen as an attempt to achieve a new kind of reconciliation among those differing value systems at a time of vigorous promotion of ideological values."(1)

The Table XXX. illustrates the organizational, professional, bureaucratic and ideological Chinese communist value system in pure or ideal form. However, there are a variety of mixes, as one moves from period to period, and from research field to research field.

In examining the patterns of institutional values as well as personality values of technical personnel emerging in post Cultural Revolution in China, one sees a dominance of ideological values, with their strong injunctions against functionally differentiated roles and institutions. Colleges and universities are not simply colleges and universities. They are rather college-factory-research institutes, or factory-research center colleges (Richard P. Suttmeier). Similarly, with reference to roles, there is an emphasis on the worker-scientist or the scientist worker ot the scientist-extension agent-peasant. The ideological values point away from careful delineations of organizations and positions with their attendant status differentials and patterns of self-interest. They point instead toward a flexible environment, characterized by norms of individual and collective initiative, co-operation, and informal communications, and by minimal organizational boundaries between research, production and educational activities. Under such conditions, an authoritative central decision-making and co-ordinating mechanism may not be necessary. " The initial post-Cultural Revolution dominance of ideological values, however, has given way to renewed interaction between the ideological value system, and the product of an earlier accomodation, the bureaucratic-professional... It is more difficult to sustain such ideologically-inspired behaviors as the hyphenated institutions or mass participation in science, in organizations committed to highly sophisticated R & D, than in institutions concerned with extention work, less sophisticated applied research, and development pertaining to lower level of technology."(2)

Table XXX.

COMPETING VALUE SYSTEMS AS THEY APPLY TO THE ORGANIZATION OF SCIENTIFIC ACTIVITIES*

A. ORGANIZATIONAL FACTORS

1. Leadership-actors making key decisions on policy, administrative and technical matters.
2. Differentiation-the extent to which roles and organizations within the science system are distinguished on the basis of specialized function.
3. Recruitment-the process of selecting new scientific and technical personnel, the criteria employed, and the control over the process.
4. Personnel mobility-the process of moving scientific and technical personnel from one job to another, the criteria employed, and the control over the process.
5. Rewards and incentives-devices used to motivate scientific and technical personnel to achieve conformity with certain kinds of incentives.
6. Project selection-the criteria employed in choosing one research or development project over another.
7. Project control-the mechanism used for overseeing the conduct of a research or developmental effort.
8. Project evaluation-the process of assessing the worth of a project, the criteria employed, the control over the process.
9. Communication-the flows of information within and between organizations within the system, between the system and user

of science and technology, and the factors affecting those flows.

10. Foreign collaboration- the relationship of the Chinese science system with science and technology in the international environment.

11. Generational relations-the nature and function of the relationships between older and younger scientific and technical personnel.

12. Extra-academic meetings-administrative and political meetings which consume time that might otherwise be invested in research and development activities.

B. PROFESSIONAL FACTORS

1. Belongs to scientists of proven ability.
2. Favoured, but on basis of skill and nature of topic.
3. Controlled by scientists and based on proven achievement.
4. Based on principle of freedom and individual interests and aspirations.
5. Colleague recognition from international scientific community; adequate material compensation.
6. Function of internal development of a field; influence of " paradigm ".
7. Flexibility exercised by competent professionals.
8. Performed by leading scientists and by scientific community generally.
9. Informal, through journals and professional meetings; opposed to secrecy.
10. Principle of non-political internationalism; advanced training in capitalist countries by many may result in de facto orientation to the West.
11. Irrelevant in principle; influence of Confucian past may result in emphasis on need for younger scientists to learn from elders.
12. Political meetings opposed as useless; grudging participation in administrative meetings.

C. BUREAUCRATIC FACTORS

1. Belongs to person of proven ability within organization.
2. Favoured, but on basis of specialization of function within network of organizations.
3. Controlled by administrators and based on organizational needs and procedures as well as achievement.
4. Administratively controlled and based on organizational needs and procedures.
5. High salaries, used to undermine salience of colleague recognition.
6. Function of needs of state as outlined by plan.
7. Exercised by administration cadres in consultation with professionals.
8. Performed by administrators with reference to plan.
9. Formalised according to organizational interests and procedures, specialized mechanisms for information transfer and control; secrecy justified.
10. Internationalism in science linked to politics (e.g. " lean to one side " in 1950s).
11. Emphasis on need for older scientists to train younger generation, need for effort to prevent elders from becoming role models for younger scientists.
12. Political meetings necessary but limited in number; administrative meetings held as organizations needs dictate; some reluctance to disrupt research routines.

D. IDEOLOGICAL FACTORS

1. Party to lead; legitimation of principle of workers and peasants playing leadership roles.
2. Opposed; scientists to become workers and vice-versa; organizational boundaries seen as impediments to release of mass initiative and effective functioning of network.

3. Controlled by Party and the masses and based on political considerations as well as achievemnt and intellectual promise.
4. Controlled by Party and includes political considerations as well as organizational needs.
5. Service to the people carries its own reward.
6. Function of close interaction of research and production.
7. Exercised by Party and masses responding to changing perceptions of production needs.
8. Performed by Party with reference to production needs and ideological criteria.
9. Informal; attacks on differentiation and organizational boundaries intended to open up communications within system.
10. Internationalist in principle; strong emphasis on native methods and wisdom (" cultural nationalism ") at times overpowers principle of internationalism.
11. Experienced scientists prized but are in need of ideological remoulding; youthful criticism of elders legitimized and encouraged as part of liberating and transforming " struggle "
12. Frequent meetings with political and administrative content since research is seen as political and political activity is seen as part of scientific progress; no hesitation to disrupt research routines.

---

* Richard P. Suttmeier, The Issue of " Institutionalization ". In: Science and Technology in the People's Republic of China. Organization for Economic Co-operation and Development, Paris, 1977, pp. 90-91.

At the macro-level these questions, especially the question of " how much self-reliance?" raise much more fundamental issues than simply that of management at the level of the enter-

prise. They reflect a broader and deeper Chinese concern with ideological transformation and social change, with Mao's continuing revolutionary struggle to transform man into a classless, unselfish, dedicated member of society, confident in his ability to solve the technological problems of development.
" The choices open to the Chinese leaders here involve conflicting values: Maoist social-revolutionary aims (ideological values) being pitted against technical-organizational imperatives (economic values). Chinese trade-off choices between these two kinds of values have fluctuated widely over time, with " ideo-logic " holding sway in periods of revolutionary fervor, such as the Great Leap and the Cultural Revolution, and " techno-logic " reassessing itself in calmer times first in the early 1960s and again after the Cultural Revolution."(3)

R E F E R E N C E S

1. Richard P. Suttmeier, ' The Issue of " Institutionalization ". In: Science and Technology in the People's Republic of China. Organization for Economic Co-operation and Development, Paris, 1977, p. 88.
2. Ibid. p. 89.
3. Hans Heyman, Jr., Kinds of Technology. Industrial Structure and Technological Advancement. In: Science and Technology in the People's Republic of China. Organization for Economic Co-operation and Development. Paris, 1977, p. 146.

S U M M A R Y

1. The antagonism between traditional Confucian human value perception and communist concept of mass-mentality and ideologized personality model is quite visible within the contemporary Chinese society.

Major factors in forming the Chinese communist personality structure and revolutionary behavior patterns are seen in a militant initiative in every undertaking, in production-related activities, in emotional stability, courage, total obedience to Party orders and guidelines, and ingeniousness in solving problems. In addition, class consciousness, selflessness, versatility and expertness in socialist construction represent additional personality values which conform to the Chinese communist doctrine and the thoughts of Mao Tse-tung, that are part of the socialization process of Chinese society. Chinese communist morality, as part of the personality structure, is based on the socialist work ethic of individuals and on a high rate of production.

The concept of the Chinese communist emotionality is part of the value system and communist personality structure. However, emotionality should not be able to determine or co-form behavior. Rationality received preference over emotional attitudes of human behavior (Schurman). Rationality however, is based on political activity, the experience of the masses, and on demostrative examples of living examples within the Party.

The hero in Communist Chinese literature is primarily a pedagogical tool for political education. The Chinese writers particularly emphasize four major personality characteristics: courage, dedication, activism and discipline. Literature in Communist China has to help to produce change (Jack Gray). Mao Tse-tung called literature one of the most important remoulding factors within the re-education program of Chinese intellectuals. Therefore, man is depicted in literature as consciously attempting to modify thought and action, which are directed toward a set of socially determined motives.

In conclusion, we may say that China has not become a country where all has been abandoned to the tenets of Marxism-Leninism-Mao Tse-tung thought. It would indeed be unrealistic to assume that within such a short period of time the ideal man and his personality characteristics would really exist (S.R. Schram).

2. The traditional Confucian personality is characterized by moderation, which means the absence of harshness, vehemence, or violence. Confucianism's operating principles are distilled from the whole body of the Classics meant for day to day guidance in the conduct of life. The following personality characteristics are extracted from ANALECTS: submissiveness to the mores, submissiveness to authority, non-competitiveness, self-respect, prudence, courage and sense of responsibility. The model person in traditional China embodied all the traits of the

ideal man. The personality values in traditional China are closely related with mystical currents of Taoism, Confucianism, and Buddhism, which proclaim a unity between individuals and some universal attribute.

3. Mao Tse-tung formed the concepts for the intellectual and ideological transformation process, as well as for the change of the human value system. The policy of letting a hundred flowers blossom and a hundred schools of thought contend offered additional guarantees for change from the traditional Chinese value system and personality characteristics to Communist ideological principles and guidelines for art and science. The basic value change within the transformation process is seen in Mao's eliminating all personal and subjective features of the traditional Confucian personality theory into a mass-oriented group personality and mentality. However, Mao Tse-tung predicted, in 1942, the failure of his revolutionary mass-line campaign in changing and remoulding the character and the personality of Chinese man. He understood the historical destiny in being unable to change the nature of man, that is, to eliminate all egoistic desires from individual human beings and to re-shape their way of thinking and behaving.

4. Marxist-Leninist political and ideological indoctrination must be carried out in all Chinese schools to indoctrinate the teachers and students with the class viewpoint of workers, the mass viewpoint, the collectivist viewpoint, the labor viewpoint or the viewpoint calling for the integration of mental labor with physical labor. Therefore, the Chinese Communist teacher has to play many roles in his career - political mentor, educator, substitute parent, family counsellor, arbiter of grades, job placement advisor and moulder of revolutionaries. " The Chinese educational psychology has to analyze the students' psychological structure of morality, and psychological laws governing the students' grip on moral ideas and the formation of their moral belief, moral sense, and moral behavior and habits; it is necessary to study the process of development of the will of the students; it is necessary to study the psychological features of self-consciousness, discipline and its formation process. However, within the past 15 years very little research about these aspects has been carried out in the People's Republic of China " (P'an Shu).

In October 1968, Mao Tse-tung issued the following educational policy directions: " Going down to do manual labor gives vast members of cadres an excellent opportunity to study once again."

The science of educational psychology and psychology in general followed the Soviet lead in the field, although some differences in emphasis and in direction of application are visible. However, one may not conclude that psychology in the People's Republic of China has established theoretical independence from the Soviet tradition or raised a challenging voice to Soviet leadership commensurate to the challenge on the political-ideological front.

5. Toward the end of 1950's, the only known study that showed concern with non-political personality characteristics, was that of Li Yi on psychological characteristics of the attitude structure of good workers and poor workers among fifth and sixth-grade pupils participating in agricultural work. It was toward the end of the recovery period from the Great Leap Forward,that truly psychological variables, rather than political ones, were used to study observable aspects of normative behavior (Robert and Ai-li S. Chin). Moral education became the most important topic of research to be developed within psychology in the early 1960s.

The scientifically oriented psychologists, who worked on psychological processes with emphasis on functions of the brain and higher nervous system, were criticized for neglecting individuality. The critics, with ideological backing, insisted that psychology should study the concrete individual, with his class background and class consciousness, and should employ the method of class analysis. However, the concept of Soviet man provided a point of departure for the Chinese concept in both its projection of the time period of human nature transformation and also in its introduction of consciousness as one of the leading features of these transformation efforts within the psychology of Chinese personality.

6. As part of the general retrenchment following the Great Leap Forward, attempts to institutionalize the ideological values were abandoned. Instead, in the effort to get the science system to work, the type of accomodation between the professional and bureaucratic systems which would have been

anticipated in 1957, but whose emergence was delayed by the promotion of ideological values, began to appear. Such an accomodation troubled the Maoists and led to the reassertion of ideological values as well as personality values of technical personnel emerging in post Cultural Revolution in China, one sees a dominance of ideological values, with their strong injunction against functionally differentiated roles and institutions. The personality values point toward a flexible environment, characterized by norms of individual and collective initiative, co-operation, minimal organizational boundaries between research, production and educational activities. The Chinese trade-off between various kinds of values have fluctuated over time, with " ideo-logic " holding sway in periods of revolutionary fervor, such as Great Leap and the Cultural Revolution, and " technocratic " reassessing itself in calmer times, first in the early 1960s and after the Cultural Revolution.

E. COMPARATIVE SUMMARY

The concept of the development of the Soviet personality structure was initiated by Lenin during the early period of the Soviet state. Since that time, the Soviet personality concept and personality values within the Marxist-Leninist ideological doctrine have undergone major changes in a variety of scientific fields and scholarly interpretations. Today, the Soviet personality structure is one of the most important subjects of scientific evaluation in the fields of philosophy, sociology, psychology, biology, management science, education and art as it relates to societal changes in conjunction with the scientific-technological revolution and in connection with the Marxist-Leninist ideological re-evaluation as well as military science. During the past several years, the subject of personality as a field of separate research has been developed in hundreds of scholarly publications and journal articles.

In comparison, the concept of the Chinese Communist personality is based on the thoughts of Mao Tse-tung and his mass-political and ideological campaigns. However, there is no scientific approach to the Chinese Communist personality structure as it exists within the Soviet social sciences. No special system of approach or application has yet been developed. The only field of direct application of personality models are the arts (literature, music, poetry) and the political-ideological doctrine.

1. The Value Concept of the Chinese Communist Personality

The Chinese Communist personality structure and its value orientation are based on the traditional Chinese personality model, which was established by the philosophy of Confucius. In addition, the Chinese Communist ideologists combined those traditional personality values with Stalinist totalitarian and early Soviet personality concepts of human existence. The traditional Confucian personality values include such personality qualities as:

1. Submissiveness to authority; which was transformed within Communist ideology into submissiveness to the Party.

2. Courage and responsibility also appear as a communist virtue and personality characteristic.
3. Esteem for the force of example; in Communist China it appears within the concept of the hero of labor who serves as a model and whose needs should be emulated.
4. Primacy of morality over specialized competence; this has been transformed in Communist China into the ideological priorities and communist morality, and political maturity as compared to any other personality qualities.
5. Non-competitiveness; as compared to competitiveness in Communist China.
6. Love of traditional learning was transformed into the study of Marxism-Leninism.

2. Chinese Communist and Traditional Soviet Personality Models

The traditional Soviet personality structure is based on totalitarian control mechanisms and complete guidance by the Communist Party of the USSR. The personality values are not developed as part of a scholarly approach or scientific system, but rather as political and ideological slogans and as a means of propaganda and political indoctrination. Primary personality concepts as value orientations can be found during the period of 1917-1960 within the Soviet society. The Chinese Communist mass-political and ideological principles of applying basic human values and personality characteristics were formulated between 1949-1978.

USSR	Communist China
1. A love for labor	1. Industrious in work
2. Continual subjugation of the individual will to that of the Party's leadership at any given time	2. Obedience to the Communist Party.

3. Patriotism	3. Courage, vigilance, sacrifice
4. A conscious sense of solidarity	4. Class consciousness
5. Collectivist, anti-egoist	5. Altruistic, cooperative with others
6. Honesty and truthfulness, moral purity and modesty, intolerance for injustice, careerism, money-grabing	6. Honesty and responsibility, prudence and forsighted, patient, diligent and persistent
7. Atheistic	7. Expresses anger or behaves aggressively only toward those who violate communist social standards or who attempt to harm the society
8. An enthusiastic contributor to the material growth of the Soviet economy	8. Ingenious in solving problems

Personality characteristics of the traditional image of the Soviet man reflect a totalitarian value orientation. The glorification of the Party's leadership and the uncritical and enthusiastic acceptance of all party orders by individual citizens has been pointed out by American scholars of Soviet affairs during the past decades (1950-1963), such as R. Bauer, T.C. Tucker, A. Inkeles, J. Kosa, F. Meyer, H. Cantril, P. Hollander, H. Swayze.

Courage, vigilance, obedience to the Party, industrious in work, collectivist, class conscious on the other hand, are slogans and propagandistic political concepts which were used by Mao Tse-tung in the early period (1949-1956) of the existence of the People's Republic of China, and which, to some degree, still exist among the ideological and political guidelines of the Chinese Communist Party. Such Chinese Communist personality values have been directly adopted from Stalinist ideological concepts and have been transplanted into the Chinese Communist mass-campaign, re-educational programs, and re-moulding campaigns in aiming at creating a new mentality and a new human value system of the Chinese citizen.

3. Contemporary Soviet and Chinese Communist Personality Concepts

The contemporary Soviet personality structure and personality values are subjects of broad scholarly research within the Soviet social sciences. The Soviet personality structure is part of the transformation process as well as re-orientation process in connection with political and ideological adjustments of the human value system to scientific-technological developments, technological innovations, and managerial capabilities. The priorities within such an ideological re-orientation or de-ideologizing process within the Soviet society are seen in individual responsibility, initiative, result-oriented social criticism, and transformed value concepts. According to the analysis of statistical data in this study, the ideological and political guidelines have lost their priority in being applied as important values of human existence. Ideology, political consciousness, and mass-propaganda are no longer the only prerequisites for a comprehensive contemporary Soviet human value system. The experimentation in applying new models and human values within the Soviet society are centered around such personality qualities elaborated in connection with social change within the Soviet society: intimacy, privacy, emotionality, criticism of social conditions, low percentage of interest in political or ideological activities, an independent leisure time structure, aesthetic activities, the ability to waste time, creative initiatives, independence at work, demanding good wages and requesting better social conditions, self-control, free choice of changing one's profession, criticizing the performance within collectives, participation in socialist competition, politeness, sense of duty, adherence to principles, integrity, strong determination, strong willpower, knowledge of technological processes, managerial abilities.

The above listed personality characteristics which have been evaluated in this study indicate human qualities common to all industrialized countries; therefore, the scholarly approach in analyzing personality qualities of Soviet citizens is similar to any other sociological or psychological investigation undertaken in Western societies. However, the results of such investigations differ. This means, that the traditional mass-political and ideological line has been replaced by advance methods of research within Soviet society changing into a technocratic society.

In comparison, the Chinese Communist contemporary development of personality structures and human values indicates a somewhat different concept and orientation. The Chinese Communist personality structure under Mao Tse-tung, and especially in recent years, has not been the subject of scholarly or scientific research within the social sciences, as in the Soviet Union. The Chinese Communist personality is characterized primarily by such qualities as emotional stability, courage, total obedience to Party orders. Additional personality values are selflessness and versatility, and militant initiative; such personality characteristics are part of the Chinese revolutionary behavior patterns which were applied and promoted since 1949.

However, there is a visible tendency towards developing personality characteristics and human values which would promote the building of a strong Chinese Communist motherland. Individuals should possess human qualities which require technical skills, scientific competence and managerial abilities. This developmental stage of personal values towards a technocratic mass-society is some 20 years behind the process already accomplished within the Soviet society. Eventually, the tendency of personality characteristics in Communist China will follow the Soviet pattern of technological competence, as well as the Western type of social dynamics of a technocratic value-oriented future society at a much lower pace, due to ideological firmness and political control systems.

Furthermore, we find a plea for admitting that people share in common certain psychological features and endevors which have been perpetuated from one society to another. This position is represented by the Soviet philosopher Tugarinov, who writes about the relationship between personality and society. In his opinion, an individual's personality is a function of his reason which depends upon his historical development, his feelings of responsibility toward society, his use of certain rights and liberties in accordance with his own like, his contribution to the growth of the society, and the manner in which his own life corresponds to the ideals of the society, or the social class to which he belongs. Such features could be found in any society in varying degrees. Tugarinov emphasized that, " the goals of personality development and its ideals can be bourgeois and communist as well. Such features are rationality, responsibility, freedom, man's possibility to think or to act by external constraint, but in accordance with his own will, individuality and dignity." (V.P. Tugarinov, Lichnost' i obshchestvo. Izdatel'stvo Mysl', Moskva, 1965, p. 61.)

4. Psychological Research on Soviet and Chinese Personalities

The current typologies of Soviet personality have, in addition to political and ideological concepts, different scientific-theoretical grounds (neurophysiological, psychophysiological, psychological, and sociological). In recent years, Soviet psychologists have analyzed a variety of personality models which are the result of their perception and the importance they ascribe to personality values; Soviet psychologists consider the personality as the apex of the mental process of man, which represents the highest level of self-orientation and self-guidance (N.I. Reynval'd). A further aspect of the psychology of the Soviet personality deals with the concept of the will in relationship to personality formation and behavior modification. The will of man forms a higher level of self-regulation and enables man the choice of free behavior and the intellectual ability to control his life (K.K. Platonov).

Contemporary social-psychological concepts of Soviet personality are expressed through the social dynamics of labor relations. However, the Soviet personality structure and the dynamics of personality formation have, in many ways, a conservative developmental tendency. The personal values of people are often determined by their emotional stability. Emotions and feelings, in comparison with general psychological concepts, have their specific regularities, which are not part of the personality structure and which are not present in every situation of life and not controlled by the will (L.V. Sokhan').

To Soviet psychologists, personality means not man in general, but a concrete individual, a member of a certain society who has complex relationships to other people. Such a concept of personality requires that the study be particularly concrete, in order to reflect the diversity of human life. It is necessary to penetrate deeper into the Soviet man's life, in order to know his activity, behavior and mind, as they are in reality (Selivanov).

In comparison to the scientific personality concepts and the broad psychological research underway in the USSR, the scholarly and professional psychological work on personality is not developed at all in the People's Republic of China. The only professional work on personality concepts was produced in the People's Republic of China at the end of the 1950s. Li Yi explored the attitude structure of good workers and poor workers among fifth and sixth-grade pupils participating in agricultural work.

Toward the end of the recovery period of the Great Leap Forward, real psychological variables, rather than political ones, were used to study observable aspects of normative behavior, formation of moral judgement and motivations for moral behavior (Ai-li Chin). Moral education became the most important topic of research to be developed within Chinese psychology in the early 1960s. The educational psychology attempted to analyze the formation of moral sense, moral faith, moral conduct, the development of the will and the formation of Communist character, effects of the collective on moral qualities and psychological characteristics of self-discipline (P'an Shu).

However, the concept of Soviet man provided a point of departure for the Chinese personality concept in both its projection of the transformation process of human nature and also in its introduction of consciousness as one of the leading features of these transformation efforts within the psychology of the personality. During the period of Chinese borrowing from Soviet scholars, Chinese psychologists had difficulties in characterizing the neurological plasticity of man. According to Munro, Chang Chih-Kuang in her study (How to Understand the Personality of Students), drew a distinction between four basic dispositional types of people: choleric, vigorous, phlegmatic, and melancholic. In addition, four neurological types differentiated by Pavlov are associated with the four dispositional types: aggressive and unrestrained, active and effective, quietly determined, weak and timid. Chang further pointed out that personalities and character can be changed under the influence of school environment, group activities, one's occupation, and the propaganda of radio and theatre.

In conclusion, one may suggest that Chinese psychological research and Chinese psychology of personality are still based on Pavlovian theories. Chinese psychologists have failed to develop their own psychological theories of value orientations; they have further failed in updating the borrowed Soviet psychological concepts of personality structures. Soviet psychologists have, since the early 1960's, developed myriad experimental approaches to personality models in attempting to change the traditional Marxist value system and Communist personality.

5. Personality Qualities of Soviet and Chinese Managers and Technical Personnel

The Soviet managers and business leaders of production collectives must understand the control mechanisms of social processes and psycho-physiological qualities of their subordinates. Additional qualifications of managers and leaders of collectives include: the coordination of material needs of people: wages, living conditions, social advancement, work performance, the authority structure of collectives and infra-personal relations among workers of collectives. The general types of leadership personalities of managers of collectives are described by Soviet scholars as: 1. The candidate should be selected to leadership positions because of objective personality characteristics, and 2. those, who share the advantages of the production process with workers of the collective. Further leadership qualities are seen as production-related technological performance, as well as social-psychological activities. The Tables XX.XXI.XXII. XXIII.XXIV. illustrate management qualities and personality characteristics of Soviet leaders of production enterprises as being: moral qualities, organizational qualities, professional qualities, and human qualities.

Leadership capabilities of Chinese managers include technological personality values, knowledge of organizational behavior and intra-system behavior (See Table XXX. on Competing Value Systems as they Apply to the Organization of Scientific Activities). The value system of Chinese technical personnel, and of managers, or leaders of production enterprises, is referred to as professional, the bureaucratic, the organizational, and the ideological personality values of managers. By comparing Tables XX. XXI. XXII. XXIII. and XXIV. on Soviet managerial abilities and personality qualities with the detailed breakdown of Chinese managerial personality qualities as shown in Table XXX., one may conclude that major value factors of the two personality concepts coincide, and that personality qualities of managers are seen to be quite similar on both sides. However, in examining the patterns of institutional values as well as personality values of technical personnel emerging in post Cultural Revolution in China, one sees a dominance of ideological personality values as a general societal characteristic.

The contemporary situation within the People's Republic of China involves conflicting values; the Maoist social-revolutionary aims (ideological values) are being pitted against technical-organizational imperatives (economic values). The choices between the two kinds of value preferences have fluctuated over time with ideological values holding sway in periods of revolutionary fervor, such as the Great Leap and the Cultural Revolution, and technological competence as well as economic efficiency of managers in calmer times: first in the early 1960's, again after the Cultural Revolution. The latter is also attributed to the Soviet technological revolution, which has been initiated under L. Brezhnev in the second part of the 1960's, in attempting to compete within the concept of the Two World Systems.

However, the future world political developments may break up the Soviet-U.S. superpower bilateralism of technological dominance and value transformation, due to the occuring technological and managerial potential being established both in Western Europe and the People's Republic of China, which can contribute to a unification of technological know-how, management abilities and personality qualities, and a general tendency towards equalization of societal characteristics throughout the world.

Such a process of value equalization has already produced significant results in the technological ability of producing nuclear weapons, through the competition in space flight technology, in the area of military technology, through international diplomacy, through the activities of multinational corporations and the desire of people to manipulate fellowman.

SELECTED BIBLIOGRAPHY

1. Agaronyan, A.S. *Zakonomernosti stanovleniya i razvitiya sotsialisticheskogo obshchestvennogo soznaniya*. " Fan ". Tashkent, 1971.
2. Andreychikov, N., *Svobodnoe vremya i razvitiye lichnosti*. Ivanovo, 1962.
3. Arkhangel'skiy, L.M., Ed., *Obshchestvennyy interes i lichnost'*. Sotsiologicheskie issledovaniya, vypusk z-y MV i SSO RSFSR. Ural'skiy gosudarstvennyy universitet imeni A.M. Gor'kogo, Sverdlovsk, 1967.
4. Arkhangel'skiy, L.M., *Sotsial'no-eticheskie problemy teorii lichnosti*. Moskva, " Mysl' ", 1974.
5. Arnold, Alfred, *Was formt die Personlichkeit?* Zur Dialektik von philosophischen und psychologischen Aspekten in der marxistisch-leninistischen Personlichkeitsauffassung. VEB Deutscher Verlag der Wissenschaften, Berlin, 1976.
6. Ascher, I., *Chinas Social Policy*. Anglo-Chinese Educational Institute, London, 1972.
7. Aseev, V.G., *Motivatsiya povedeniya i formirovanie lichnosti*. Izdatel'stvo " Mysl' ", Moskva, 1976.
8. Babosov, E.M., Ed., *Kommunizm i formirovanie nauchnogo mirovozzreniya mass*. Izdatel'stvo " Vysheyshaya Shkola Minsk ", 1966.
9. Balakin, I.F., Ed., *Problemy cheloveka sovremennoy filosofii*. Moskva, Nauka, 1969.
10. Barbu, Z., *Democracy and Dictatorship, their Psychology and Patterns of Life*. New York, Grove Press, 1956.
11. Bauer, R.A., *The New Man in Soviet Psychology*. Harvard University Press, Cambridge, 1952.
12. Baykov, V.G., Ed., *Svobodnoe vremya i vsestoronnee razvitie lichnosti*. Izdatel'stvo " Mysl' ", Moskva, 1965.
13. Bertsch, G.K., *Comparative Communism, The Soviet, Chinese and Yugoslav Models*. Freeman and Company, San Francisco, 1976.

14. Birch, C., Ed., Chinese Communist Literature. Praeger, New York, 1963.

15. Bolgov, V.I., Vnerabochee vremya i uroven' zhizni trudyashchisya. Akademiya Nauk SSSR Sibirskoe otdelenie, Institut ekonomiki i organizatsii promyshlennogo proizvodstva, Novosibirsk, 1964.

16. Borovskiy, M.I., Determinizm i nravstvennoe povedenie lichnosti. Nauka i tekhnika, Minsk, 1974.

17. Bozhovich, L.I., Slavina, L.S., Fifty Years of Soviet Psychology of Upbringing. Voprosy Psikhologii, 1967, 13 (5), pp. 51-70. In: Josef Brozek and Dan I. Slobin, Psychology in the USSR: An Historical Perspective. International Arts and Sciences Press, Inc., White Plains, New York, 1968.

18. Bronfenbrenner, Y., Soviet Studies of Personality Development and Socialism. In: Bauer, R., Ed., Some Views on Soviet Psychology, American Psychological Association, Washington, D.C., 1962.

19. Brozek, J., Slobin, D.I., Ed., Psychology in the USSR. International Arts and Sciences Press, Inc., White Plains, New York, 1972.

20. Byrne, D., Ed., Personality Research. Prentice-Hall, Inc., Englewood Cliffs, New Jersey, 1966.

21. Cantril, H., Soviet Leaders and Mastery over Man. Rutgers University Press, New Brunswick, 1960.

22. Chai Ch'u, The Changing Society of China. A Mentor Book, Published by the New American Library, 1962.

23. Chelovek, Obshchestvo, religiya. Ed., Ivanov, A.S., Kichanova, I.M., Kurochkin, P.K., Moskva, " Mysl' ", 1968.

24. Chen, Hsi-en T., Thought Reform of the Chinese Intellectuals. Hong Kong University Press, 1960.

25. Chesnokov, D., Karpushin, V., Man and Society (Lichnost' i obshchestvo), Progress Publishers, Moscow, 1966.

26. Chin, Robert and Ai-li, Psychological Research in Communist China, 1949-1966. The MIT Press, Cambridge, 1969.

27. Cole, M., Ed., A Handbook of Contemporary Soviet Psychology. Basic Books, Inc., Publishers, N.Y. 1969.

28. Compton, B., Mao's China: Party Reform Documents, 1942-1944. University of Washington Press, Seattle, 1966.

29. Dautov, T.M., Lichnost' kak sotsialisticheskaya problema. Nauka, Alma-Ata, 1970.

30. Davlekeldiyev, Ed., Ideologiya i obshchestvennaya psikhologiya. Akademiya Nauk Kirgiskoy SSR, Institut Filosofii i prava, Izdatel'stvo ILIM, Frunze, 1968.

31. De Bary, W.T., Individualism and Humanitarianism in Late Ming Thought. In: Self and Society in Ming Thought, Columbia University Press, New York, 1970.

32. Demin, M.V., Problemy teorii lichnosti. Izdatel'stvo Moskovskogo universiteta, Moskva, 1977.

33. Druee, H., Psychologie aus dem Begriff Hegels Personlichkeitstheorie. Walter de Gruyter, Berlin, 1976.

34. Dryakhlov, N.I. Ed., Nauchno-tekhnicheskaya revolutsiya i osobennosti sotsial'nogo razvitiya v sovremennuyu epokhu. Izdatel'stvo Moskovskogo universiteta, Moskva, 1974.

35. Dunn, S.P., Ed., Sociology in the USSR. International Arts and Sciences Press, Inc., White Plains, N.Y. 1969.

36. Eng-Liedmeier, van der, A.M., Soviet Literary Characters. An investigation into the portrayal of Soviet Man in Russian prose, 1917-1953. Mouton & Co., Gravenhage, 1959.

37. Elizar'yev, E.A., Vremya obshchestva. Filosofskiy i sotsial'no-ekonomicheskiy aspekt; Izdatel'stvo Nauka, Sibirskoe otdelenie, Novosibirsk, 1969.

38. Elmeyev, V.Ya., Kommunizm i razvitie cheloveka kak proizvoditel'noy sily obshchestva. Izdatel'stvo sotsial'no-ekonomicheskoy literatury, " Mysl' ", Moskva, 1964.

39. Ermilov, V.V., Literatura i novyy chelovek. Akademiya Nauk SSSR, Institut mirovoy literatury, imeni A.A. Gor'kogo, Moskva, 1963, Izdatel'stvo Akademii Nauk SSSR.

40. Ermolaev, H., Soviet Literary Theories, 1917-1934. A Genesis of Social Realism. University of California Publications in Modern Philology, University of California Press, Berkeley and Los Angeles, 1963.

41. Filipov, F.P., Ed., Voprosy razvitiya sotsialisticheskogo obshchestva. Sbornik statey, Sverdlovsk, 1971.

42. Fleron, F.J., Kelly, R.M., Personality, Behavior and Communist Ideology. In: Hoffman, E.P., Fleron, F.J., The Conduct of Soviet Foreign Policy. Aldine-Atherton, Chicago, New York, 1971.

43. Fokkema, D.W., Literary Doctrine in China and Soviet Influence, 1956-1960. Mouton & Co., The Hague, 1965.

44. Formirovanie novogo cheloveka, stroitelya kommunizma. Ministerstvo narodnogo obrazovaniya MSSR, Kishinevskiy ordena trudovogo krasnogo znamenya, Gosudarstvenniy universitet im. V.I. Lenina, Izdatel'stvo Shtiintsa, Kishinev, 1973.

45. Fraser, S.E., Ed., Education and Communism. Pall Mall Press, London, 1971.

46. Fraser, S.E., Chinese Communist Education. Records of the First Decade. Vanderbilt University Press, Nashville, 1965.

47. Frenkel', I.A., Voprosy psikhologii lichnosti i kollektivi shkol'nikov i studentov. Irkutsk, 1974.

48. Furth, C., Ting Wen-Chiang, Sciences and China's New Culture. Harvard University Press, Cambridge, 1970.

49. Gak, G.M., Dialektika kollektivnosti i individual'nosti. Izdatel'stvo " Mysl' ", Moskva, 1967.

50. Gerulaities, R., Ed., Oakland Symposium on Socialist Realism in Literature. Oakland University, Rochester, Michigan, 1975.

51. Glazachev, A.A., Svobodnoe vremya i vsestoronnee razvitie lichnosti. Polit. samoobrazovanie, Moskva, 1960.

52. Glazachev, A.A., Trud i vsestoronnee razvitie lichnosti. Izdatel'stvo " Mysl' ", Moskva, 1968.

53. Glotochkin, A.D., Fedenko, N.F., Shelyag, V.V., Ed., Problemy psikhologii voinskogo kollektiva. Voennoe Izdatel'stvo Ministerstva Oborony SSSR, Moskva, 1973.

54. Gorshkov, V.A., Puti povysheniya tvorcheskoy initsiativy i aktivnosti narodnykh mass. Mariyskoe knizhnoe izdatel'stvo Yoshkar-Ola, 1967, Povolzhskiy lesotekhnicheskiy institut imeni M. Gor'kogo.

55. Granin, D.M., Ed., Lichnost' i obshchestvo. Ministerstvo vysshego i srednedo spetsial'nogo obrazovaniya RSFSR, Kaliningradskiy gosudarstvennyy universitet, Kaliningrad, 1976.

56. Gray, J., Chinese Communism in Crisis. Maoism and Cultural Revolution. Praeger, New York, 1968.

57. Grushin, B., Svobodnoe vremya. " Mysl' ", Moskva, 1967.

58. Hierschke, A., Konturen und Perspektiven, zum Menschenbild in der Gegenwartsliteratur in der Sowjetunion. Berlin, Akademie Verlag, 1969.

59. Hinz, E., Die Geburt des neuen Menschen; Tendenzen in der modernen sowjetischen Literatur. Frankfurt am Main, Sinnva Verlag, 1966.

60. Hollander, P., Models of behavior in Stalinist Literature. A Case Study of Totalitarian Values and Controls. American Sociological Review, 1964, pp. 352-364.

61. Hollander, P., A Reader in Comparative Sociology and Perception. Prentice-Hall, Inc., Englewood Cliffs, New Jersey.

62. Honigman, J., Personality and Culture. Harper and Row Publishers, New York, 1967.

63. Horz, H.E., Blickpunkt Personlichkeit. Ein Beitrag der Ethik zur Theorie und Praxis der Personlichkeitsentwicklung. VEB Deutscher Verlag der Wissenschaften, Berlin, 1975.

64. Hough, J.F., The Soviet Union and Social Sciences Theory. Russian Research Center Studies 77, Harvard University Press, Cambridge, 1977.

65. Houn, F.W., To Change a Nation. Propaganda and Indoctrination in Communist China. The Free Press of Glencoe and Bureau of Social and Political Research, Michigan State University, 1961.

66. Hsiung, Chieh, J., Ideology and Practice. The Evolution of Chinese Communism. Praeger, New York, 1970.

67. Hsiung, Chieh, J., The Logic of Maoism. Praeger, N.Y. 1974.

68. Hsueh-Wen, Wang, Chinese Communist Education; The Yenan Period. Institute of International Relations, Republic of China, 1975.

69. Hu, Ming Shi, Toward a New World Outlook. AMS Press, Inc., New York, 1976.

70. Hunt, R., Ed., Personalities and Cultures. The Natural History Press, New York, 1967.

71. Hunter, E., Brain-Washing in Red China. The Vanguard Press, Inc., New York, 1971.

72. Inkeles, A., Social Change in Soviet Russia. Simon and Schuster, New York, 1971.

73. Inkeles, A., Bauer, R., The Soviet Citizen. Daily Life in a Totalitarian Society. Atheneum, New York, 1968.

74. Issledovaniya myshleniya v sovetskoy psikhologii. Akademiya Nauk SSSR, Institut Filosofii, Izdatel'stvo Nauka, Moskva, 1966.

75. Ivanov, V., Ideyno-esteticheskie printsipi sovteskoy literatury. Izdatel'stvo khudozhestvennaya literatura, Moskva, 1971.

76. Jojic, B., Covek u socijalizmu.Ustavne koncepcije prava coveka i njegove zastite u evropskim socijalistickim zemljama, IMPP, Institu za medjunarodni radnicki pokret, Beograd, 1972.

77. Kaganov, A., Kharaktery i obstoyatel'stva sovetskoy literatury. Sovetskiy pisatel', Moskva, 1959.

78. Kaidalov, D.P., Zakon peremeny truda i vsestoronnee razvitie cheloveka. " Mysl' ", Moskva, 1968.

79. Kalinin, A.I., Ed., Razvitie lichnosti v usloviyakh stroitel'stva kommunizma. Ministerstvo vysshego i srednego spetsial'nogo obrazovaniya RSFSR, Chuvashskiy gosudarstvennyy universitet im. I.N. Ul'yanova, Cheboksary, 1970.

80. Khrushchev, N.S., The Great Mission of Literature and Art. Progress Publishers, Moscow, 1964.

81. Kirillova, M.V., Education as a Factor of all-round Development of the Personality in the Soviet Society. Institut of Philosophy of the Academy of Social Sciences of the Ukrainian SSR. Kharkov State University.

82. Kollektiv i lichnost'. Ministerstvo vysshego i srednogo spetsial'nogo obrazovaniya RSFSR, Irkutskiy gosudarstvennyy universitet imeni A.A. Zhdanova, Irkutsk, 1972.

83. Kollektiv i lichnost'. Akademiya obshchestvennykh nauk pri TsK KPSS, Izdatel'stvo " Mysl' ", Moskva, 1968.

84. Kommunizm i lichnost'. Ed., Chesnokov, D.I., Izdatel'stvo politicheskoy literatury, Moskva, 1964.

85. Kon, I.S., Sotsiologiya lichnosti. Izdatel'stvo politicheskoy literatury, Moskva, 1967.

86. Konstantinov, F.V., Ed., Lichnost' pri sotsializme. Nauka, Moskva, 1969.

87. Konturen und Perspektiven zum Menschenbild in der Gegenwartsliteratur in der sowjetischen und Deutschen Demokratischen Republik. Akademie Verlag, Berlin, 1969.

88. Korneyev, M.A., Problemy sotsial'noy tipologii lichnosti. Izdatel'stvo Leningradskogo universiteta, Leningrad, 1971.

89. Korshunova, V.V., Dialekticheskoe edinstvo individual'no-psikhologicheskikh osobenostey i obshchestvennykh chert lichnosti. Izdatel'stvo L'vovskogo universiteta, 1967.

90. Kosa, J., Two Generations of Soviet Man. A Study in the Psychology of Communism. The University of North Carolina Press, 1962.

91. Kotov, L.I., Vospitanie novogo cheloveka. Sbornik statey. Izdatel'stvo Udmurtiya, Izhevsk, 1964.

92. Kovalyov, S., O natsional'noy gordosti sovetskikh lyudey. Gospolitizdat, Moskva, 1950.

93. Kovalyov, S.M., O cheloveke, ego poraboshchenii i osvobozhdenii. Izdatel'stvo politicheskoy literatury, Moskva, 1970.

94. Kovalev, V.A., Utverzhdayushchiy kharakter sovetskoy literatury. Izdatel'stvo Akademii Nauk SSSR, Moskva, 1960.

95. Kreusler, A.A., Contemporary Education and Moral Upbringing in the Soviet Union. University Microfilm International, 1976.

96. Kryazhev, P., Obshchestvo i lichnost'. Gospolitizdat, Moskva, 1964.

97. Krylov, A.A., Kuz'min, E.S., Ed., Psikhologiya - proizvodstvu i vospitaniya. Izdatel'stvo Leningradskogo universiteta, Leningrad, 1977.

98. Krjazev, P.E., Die Personlichkeit im Sozialismus. Akademie Verlag, Berlin, 1972.

99. Kupper, H., Some Psychological Hypothesis on Mao Tse-tungs Personality. In: Studies in Comparative Communism, VII, 1-2, 1974.

100. Kvetna, M.S., Ed., Formirovanie cheloveka komm.obshchestva. Sbornik nauchnikh statey, Kuibyshev, 1971.

101. Kuszynski, J., Indiwidualnosc i ojeczyzna. Panstwowy Institut i Wydanieczy, Warszawa, 1972.

102. Kultschinskij, A., Die Marxistisch-sowjetische Konzeption des Menschen im Lichte der Westlichen Psychologie. Institut zur Erforschung der UDSSR, Munchen, Serie I., No. 32, Nov. 1956.

103. Kuz'min, E.S., Volkov, I.P., Ed., Rukovoditel' i kollektiv. Sotsial'no-psikhologicheskiy ocherk, Lenizdat, 1974.

104. Kuz'minov, G.A., Chustvennoe i logicheskoe v vospitanii mikromira. Akademiya obshchestvennykh nauk pri TsK KPSS, Kafedra filosofii, Izdatel'stvo " Mysl' ", Moskva, 1965.

105. Lammers, R., An analysis of a representative sample of plays, written and used for propaganda purposes by the Chinese Communists. Ph.D. Thesis, University of Minnesota, 1962. University Microfilms, Michigan.

106. Lavrinenko, V.N., Sotsiologicheskie problemy lichnosti. Krasnoyarsk, STI, 1973.

107. Levenson, J.R., Confucian China and its Modern Fate. The Problems of Intellectual Continuity. University of California Press, Berkeley and Los Angeles, 1958.

108. Levitas, M., Marxist perspectives in the sociology of education. Routledge & Kegan Paul, London, 1974.

109. Levy,M.J., The Family Revolution in Modern China. Octagon Books, New York, 1963.

110. Lewis, J.W., Leadership in Communist China. Ithaca, Cornell University Press, 1963.

111. Lichnost' pri sotsializme. Akademiya Nauk SSSR. Institut Filosofii, Izdatel'stvo Nauka, Moskva, 1968.

112. Lichnost', obshchestvo i gosudarstvo. Akademiya obshchestvennykh nauk SSSR, Institut gosudarstva i prava, Izdatel'stvo Nauka, Moskva, 1966.

113. Lifton, R.J., Thought Reform and the Psychology of Totalism. W.W. Norton & Company, Inc., New York, 1963.

114. Likhachev, I., Nravstvennoe razvitie lichnosti v kollektivakh komm. truda. Krasnoyarskoe knizhnoe izdatel'stvo, Krasnoyarsk, 1963.

115. Lin, W.T., Chinese Society under Communism. Wiley, New York, 1967.

116. Liszki, J. Ed., Czlowiek Socjalizm, Revolucja Naukowo-Techniczna. Ksiazka i Wiedza, Warszawa, 1974.

117. Litvinov, L.N., Trud i byt kak faktory formirovaniya lichnosti. Prioskoe knizhnoe izdatel'stvo, Tula, 1973.

118. Lu, A., Ya-li, Political Control of Literature in Communist China. 1949-1966. Ph.D. Thesis, Indiana University, 1972.

119. Macfarquhar, R., The Hundred Flowers Campaign and the Chinese Intellectuals. Praeger Publishers, New York, 1960.

120. Mal'skiy, S.P., Nauka i vsestoronnee razvitie lichnosti. Izdatel'stvo " Shtiintsa ", Kishinev, 1974

121. Mao Tse-tung, Talks at the Yenan Forum on Art and Literature. Foreign Language Press, Peking, 1960.

122. Markov, M., Socialisticeskie obshchestveni otnoshenija. Izdatel'stvo na BKP, Sofija, 1970.

123. Maslov, P.P., Sotsiologiya i statistika. Moskva, 1967.

124. Mathewson, R.W., The Russian Positive Hero. Columbia University Press, New York, 1964.

125. McLeish, J., Soviet Psychology, History, Theory, Content. Methuen and Co., Ltd., London, 1975.

126. Mel'nikov, G.I., Lichnost' i kollektiv. Irkutskiy gosudarstvennyy universitet imeni A.A. Zhdanova, Irkutsk, 1972.

127. Meyer, F.S., The Moulding of Communists. A Harvest Book, 1961.

128. Mokronosov, G.V., Ed., Lichnost' i obshchestvo. Ministerstvo vysshego i srednego spetsial'nogo obrazovaniya RSFSR. Ural'skiy ordena trudovogo krasnogo znameni politicheskikh institut imeni S.M. Kirova, Sverdlovsk, 1967.

129. Molodykh, V.I., Vsestoronnee razvitie lichnosti i nauchno-tekhnicheskoe tvorchestvo rabochikh. Ural'skiy gosudarstvennyy universitet imeni A.M. Gor'kogo, Sverdlovsk, 1965.

130. Morgunov, I.G., Vsestoronnee razvitie lichnosti. Izdatel'stvo Liesma, Riga, 1967.

131. Muensterberger, W., Orality and Dependence: Characteristics of Southern Chinese. In: Psychoanalysis and the Social Sciences, 3. (1951), 37-69.

132. Munro, D.J., The Concept of Man in Contemporary China. The University of Michigan Press, Ann Arbor, 1977.

133. Myalikin, A., Svobodnoe vremya i vsestoronnee razvitie lichnosti. Izdatel'stvo Vysshey Shkoli pri TsK KPSS, Mos kva, 1962.

134. Nadol'nyy, I.F., Lazarenko, E.V., Sotsializm i lichnost'. Izdatel'skoe ob'edinenie " Vyshcha Shkola ", Golovnoe Izdatel'stvo, Kiev, 1976.

135. Niel, M., Psychoanalyse du Marxisme. Le Courier du Livre, Paris, 1967.

136. Nikishov, S.I., Ed., Nauchno-tekhnicheskaya revolutsiya i osobenosti sotsial'nogo razvitiya v sovremennuyu epokhu. Izdatel'stvo Moskovskogo universiteta, 1974.

137. Nikolaev, L.V., Ob'yektivnie i sub'yektivnie faktory sotsial'nogo progressa i svobody. Izdatel'stvo Moskovskogo universiteta, Moskva, 1974.

138. Nikolaichev, B.O., Osoznavaemoe i neosoznavaemoe v nravstvennom povedenii lichnosti. Izdatel'stvo Moskovskogo universiteta, Moskva, 1976.

139. Novyy chelovek, novyy gumanizm. Ed., Lomidze, G.I., Akademiya obshchestvennykh nauk pri TsK KPSS, Izdatel'stvo " Mysl' ", Moskva, 1969.

140. Present-day Russian Psychology. Ed., O'Connor, N., Pergamon Press, Oxford, 1966.

141. Orleans, L.A., Professional Manpower and Education in Communist China. NSF-61-3, 1961, Washington, D.C.

142. Orlov, G.P., Svobodnoe vremya kak sotsiologicheskaya kategoriya. Ministerstvo vysshego spetsial'nogo obrazovaniya RSFSR, Sverdlovskiy Yuridicheskiy institut, Sverdlovsk, 1973.

143. Orzikh, M.F., Lichnost' i pravo. Yuridicheskoe izdatel'stvo, Moskva, 1975.

144. Osborn, R., Marxism and Psychoanalysis. Bornie and Rockliff, London, 1965.

145. Otto, K., Psychologische Untersuchungen zur Entwicklung sozialistischer Personlichkeiten. Volk und Wissen, Volkseigener Verlag, Berlin, 1971.

146. Payne, T.R., S.L. Rubinsteyn and the philosophical foundations of Soviet psychology. D. Reidel Publishing Company, Dordrecht, Holland, 1969.

147. Perfil'yev, M.N., Obshchestvennye otnosheniya. Akademiya Nauk SSSR, Leningradskaya Kafedra Filosofii, Izdatel'stvo Nauka, Leningradskoe Otdelenie, Leningrad, 1974.

148. Personlichkeit. In: Sowjetsystem und Demokratische Gesellschaft, Eine Vergleichende Enzyklopedie, Band V, Herder Verlag, Freiburg, 1972.

149. Petrosyan, G.S., Vnerabochee vremya trudyashchisya v SSSR. Ekonomika, Moskva, 1965.

150. Pismenova, V.N., Svobodnoe vremya v sotsialisticheskom obshchestve. Nauka, Moskva, 1974.

151. Platonov, K.K., Lichnost' i trud. Akademiya Nauk SSSR, Institut Filosofii, Izdatel'stvo " Mysl' ", Moskva, 1965.

152. Platonov, K.K., O chertakh lichnosti novogo rabochego. Akademiya Nauk SSSR, Institut Filosofii, Izdatel'stvo Akademii Nauk, SSSR, Moskva, 1963.

153. Price, R.F., Marx and Education in Russia and China. Croom Helen, London, 1977.

154. Price, R.F., Education in Communist China. Praeger, New York, 1970.

155. Problemy formirovaniya komm. soznaniya lichnosti. Ed., Chernyak, V., Akademiya Nauk Kazakhskoy SSR, Nauka, Alma-Ata, 1972.

156. Prokof'yev, V.I., Kodeks komm. morali i religioznaya " nravstvennost' ". Voennoe izdatel'stvo Ministerstva Oborony SSSR, Moskva, 1964.

157. Prudenskiy, G.A., Ed., Vnerabochee vremya trudyashchisya. Akademiya Nauk SSSR, Sibirskoe otdelenie, Institut ekonomiki i organisatsii promyshlennogo proizvodstva, Novosibirsk, 1961.

158. Pye, L.W., The Spirit of Chinese Politics. A Psychological Study of the Authority Crisis in Political Development. The MIT Press, Cambridge, 1970.

159. Rahmani, L., Soviet Psychology. International University Press,Inc., New York, 1973.

160. Reynval'd, N.I., Lichnost' kak predmet psikhologicheskogo analiza. Vysshaya Shkola, Kharkov, 1974.

161. Ridley, C.P., Doolin, D.J., The Making of a Model Citizen in Communist China. The Hoover Institution Press, Stanford, 1971.

162. Rogov, I.M., Nauchno-tekhnicheskiy progress i razvitie lichnosti. Lenizdat, 1974.

163. Rostow, W.W., A Comparison of Russian and Chinese Societies under Communism. Cambridge, Center for International Studies, MIT, 1955.

164. Rot, N., Psihologija licnosti. Zavod za izdavanje Udjbenika Socialisticke Republike Srbije, Beograd, 1969.

165. Rumyantsev, V.M., Protivorechiya v razvitii lichnosti i ikh razreshenie v protsesse vospitaniya. Kalinin, 1972.

166. Ruhle, J., Literatur und Revolution. Kiepenheuer und Witsch, Koln, 1960.

167. Ryabov, D.D., Sotsial'no gosudarstvo i vospitanie novogo cheloveka. Izdatel'stvo Moskovskogo universiteta, Moskva, 1972.

168. Sabirov, Kh.F., Voprosy sotsial'nogo razvitiya lichnosti. Kazan', 1973.

169. Sarsenbayev, T., Sotsializm i svoboda lichnosti. Izdatel'stvo Kazakhstan, Alma-Ata, 1969.

170. Schram, S.R., Ed., Authority Participation and Cultural Change in China. Cambridge University Press, 1973.

171. Schurman, F., Ideology and Organization in Communist China. University of California Press, Berkeley and Los Angeles, 1971.

172. Seifmar, E.,Shi Ming Hu, Toward a New World Outlook. A Documentary History of Education in the People's Republic of China, 1949-1976. AMS Press, Inc., New York, 1977.

173. Semenov, O.G., Ed., Sotsial'naya psikhologiya lichnosti. Obshchestvo ' Znanie ', RSFSR, Leningradskaya organisatsiya, Leningrad, 1974.

174. Seve, L., Marxisme et theorie de la Personalite. Editions sociales, Paris, 1969.

175. Seybolt, P.J., Revolutionary Education in China. Documents and Commentary. International Arts and Sciences Press, Inc., White Plains, New York.

176. Shkerin, M., Sovetskiy kharakter. Literaturno-kriticheskie stat'i. Sovetskiy pisatel', Moskva, 1963.

177. Schneidman, N.N., Literature and Ideology in Soviet Education. Published for the Centre for Russian and East European Studies, University of Toronto, Lexington Books, 1973.

178. Simon, B., Ed., Psychology in the Soviet Union. Stanford University Press, Stanford, 1957.

179. Smelser, N.J., Personality and Social System. John Wiley and Sons, Inc., New York, 1963.

180. Sokhan', L.V., Dukhovnyy progress lichnosti i kommunizm. Akademiya Nauk Ukrainskoy SSR, Institut Filosofii, Naukova Dumka, Kiev, 1966.

181. Sokolov, E.V., Kul'tura i lichnost'. Akademiya Nauk SSSR, Institut Filosofii Leningradskogo Sektora, Izdatel'stvo Nauka, Leningrad, 1972.

182. Solomon, R.H., Mao's Revolution and the Chinese Political Culture. University of California Press, Berkeley, 1972.

183. Spasibenko, S.G., Lichnost' i sotsializm. Izdatel'stvo Vysshaya Shkola, Moskva, 1972.

184. Starr, J.B., Continuing the Revolution, The Political Thought of Mao. Princeton University Press, 1979.

185. Steinert, H., Die Strategien sozialen Handelns; Zur Soziologie der Personlichkeit und Sozialization. Juventa Verlag, Munchen, 1972.

186. Stempkovskaya, V.I., Sotsializm i svoboda. Nauka, Moskva, 1975.

187. Stroitel'stvo kommunizma i dukhovnyy mir cheloveka. Izdatel'stvo Nauka, Moskva, 1966.

188. Stroitel'stvo kommunizma i formirovanie lichnosti. Ed., Antonenko, V.G., Ordena Trudovogo Krasnogo znameni, Izdatel'stvo Politicheskoy Literatury Ukrainy, Kiev, 1976.

189. Strukov, E., Kommunizm i vsestoronnee razvitie lichnosti. Izdatel'stvo Znanie, Moskva, 1960.

190. Struve, G., Soviet Russian Literature, 1917-1950. University of Oklahoma Press, 1951.

191. Suttmeier, R.P., Research and Revolution. Science Policy and Societal Change in China. Lexington Books, Lexington, Mass. 1974.

192. Suttmeier, R.P., The Issue of " Institutionalization ". In: Science and Technology in the People's Republic of China. Organization for Economic Co-operation and Development. 1977.

193. Swayze, H., Political Control of Literature in the USSR, 1946-1959. Harvard University Press, 1962.

194. Sychev, Yu.V., Mikrosreda i lichnost'. Akademiya obshchestvennykh nauk pri TsK KPSS, Kafedra marksistko-leninskoy filosofii, Izdatel'stvo " Mysl' ", Moskva, 1974.

195. Tadevosyan, V.S., Lichnost', obshchestvo i gosudarstvo. Nauka, Moskva, 1966.

196. Tsi-an Hsia, The Gate of Darkness. Studies on Leftist Literary Movement in China. University Press of Washington, 1968.

197. Tucker, R.C., Stalin and the Uses of Psychology. U.S. Air Force Project, RAND, Research Memorandum, RM 1441, March 1955.

198. Tucker, R.C. The Soviet Political Mind. Studies in Stalinism and Post-Stalin Change. Praeger, New York, 1963.

199. Tugarinov, V., Lichnost' i obshchestvo. " Mysl' ", Moskva, 1965.

200. Vaugham, C.J., Soviet Socialist Realism. Origins and Theory. St. Martins Press, New York, 1974.

201. Wallace, G.R., Context for Soviet Education Today.MSS Information Corporation, New York, 1974.

202. Wang, C.K.S., The Control of Teachers in Communist China. A Socio-Political Study. Air Force Personnel and Training Center, Lackland Air Force Base, Texas, 1955.

203. Weakland, J.H., The Organization of Action in Chinese Culture. In: Psychiatry, 13 (1950), 361-370.

204. Wright, A.F., Ed., Confucian Personalities. Stanford University Press, Stanford, 1962.

205. Yang, C.K., The Chinese Family in the Communist Revolution. Cambridge, MIT Press, 1959.

206. Yarmolinskiy, A., Literature under Communism. Russian and East European Series, Russian and East European Institut, Indiana University, Vol. 20.

207. Yaroshevskiy, T., Mansurov, N.S. Ed., Aktivnost' lichnosti v sotsialisticheskom obshchestve. Akademiya Nauk SSR, Institut sotsiologicheskikh issledovanii, Izdatel'stvo Nauka, Moskva, 1976.

208. Zhuravlev, V.V., Problemy duhovnoy zhizni obshchestva. Izdatel'stvo Rostovskogo universiteta, Rostov na Donu, 1972.

AUTHOR AND SUBJECT INDEX